AGRICULTURAL SCIENCE
for the
CARIBBEAN

3

Ralph Persad

OXFORD
UNIVERSITY PRESS

OXFORD
UNIVERSITY PRESS

Great Clarendon Street, Oxford, OX2 6DP, United Kingdom

Oxford University Press is a department of the University of Oxford.
It furthers the University's objective of excellence in research, scholarship,
and education by publishing worldwide. Oxford is a registered trade mark of
Oxford University Press in the UK and in certain other countries

First published by Thomas Nelson and Sons Ltd in 1978
This edition published by Oxford University Press in 2014

British Library Cataloguing in Publication Data
Data available

978-0-17-566396-5

21

Printed by CPI Group (UK) Ltd, Croydon CR0 4YY

Acknowledgements

The author and publishers are grateful to the following for
permission to use photographs in this book:
Chaguaramas Agricultural Development Project: pages 64, 65 (top
left, centre left and right, bottom right), 70, 72 (top right, bottom)
Joe Clarke: page 85
Farmer's Weekly: pages 111, 116
Franklyn Holder of Norton's Studio: pages 10, 14, 16, 18, 20, 72 (top
left, left margin), 83, 86, 88, 95 (top), 96, 99, 103, 117, 118, 128, 129,
132, 136, 137, 145, 160, 161
Massey-Ferguson: pages 65 (top right), 73
Ministry of Agriculture, Trinidad: page 162
David Simson: pages 30, 40, 65 (bottom left), 87, 172, 176, 177, 178,
179
John Topham Picture Library: page 100

Although we have made every effort to trace and contact all
copyright holders before publication this has not been possible in all
cases. If notified, the publisher will rectify any errors or omissions at
the earliest opportunity.

Contents

Preface

Agricultural Science is an integral component of the curriculum of our primary, junior secondary, composite, senior comprehensive and many senior secondary schools This three-book series for junior secondary and middle school classes in the Caribbean, has been prepared as an observational/activity-oriented course, and is intended to assist teachers in their agricultural programmes through the encouragement in the pupil of an enquiring and practical attitude toward the subject.

To make the best use of this series it is essential that the teacher should read and study the lessons well in advance so that he/she can prepare the necessary teaching aids and experiments, both of which are vital in the effective teaching of Agricultural Science.

Pupils should be encouraged to investigate and find out more about agriculture in their own localities, and to keep careful records of their findings.

Most of the chapters are designed for teachers to begin their lessons with observations, followed by discussions, inferences, and the application of these inferences in agricultural practices. Practical activity is an essential part of this exercise.

The school garden should be established. This should contain plants and features that can be used for reference and study purposes. Field trips and demonstrations all help to make the teaching programme more effective and stimulating.

Every attempt should be made to integrate the agricultural studies with those of the general science and social studies programmes, as well as any other allied subject in the school curriculum.

Though teachers should find the text adequate, they should feel free to adapt the lesson material to suit their own locality and interest, and to supplement the text with any further reading material that they may consider relevant and helpful.

R.S.P.
October 1993

1 The propagation of garden plants

Lesson objectives

Many garden plants are propagated artificially. On completing this lesson you should be able to:

1 List four artificial methods of plant propagation.

2 Select, prepare and propagate stem cuttings in a propagator.

3 Propagate plants by means of air layering.

4 State the principles of budding and grafting and describe the steps involved in the budding and grafting process.

5 State the advantages gained by the use of budded and grafted plants.

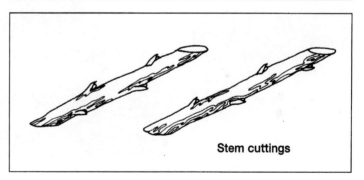

Stem cuttings

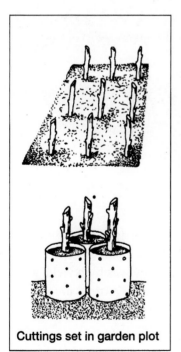

Cuttings set in garden plot

In Book One we learnt that many ornamental and garden plants are propagated vegetatively by means of stem cuttings. However, not all plants grow readily by simply placing stem cuttings in the soil. The cuttings of some plants will only set roots under special conditions provided in a **plant propagator**.

You can construct a simple plant propagator in your school. The diagrams on page 2 show you how to do this.

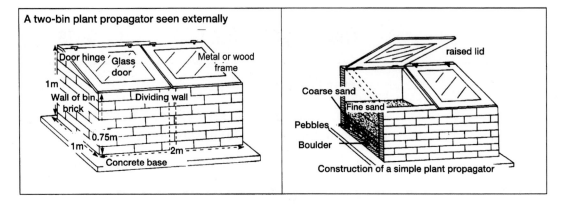

A two-bin plant propagator seen externally

Construction of a simple plant propagator

The plant propagator

These pictures were taken at a cocoa propagation unit. Notice the glass houses in which special bins are constructed for propagating plants. Some of these bins are filled with a rooting medium such as sand or fibre-bast whilst some of them are empty and are used for rooting potted plants or for hardening potted plants that have already been rooted.

Propagation unit for cocoa

A propagating bin

How to grow plants in a propagator

Taking cuttings

The propagator is used chiefly for propagating plants from cuttings. The cuttings are taken from matured parent trees that show desirable characteristics such as high yield, good quality fruit, and resistance to disease. Cuttings are usually taken in the early morning and placed in a container with water.

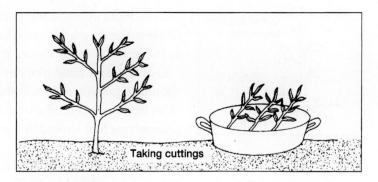

Taking cuttings

Preparing cuttings

Cuttings are prepared to a length of 20–25 cm. The lower leaves are pruned as close as possible to the stem and the remaining three or four leaves at the top are reduced to half their size. The stems are given a clean, sharp cut to an angle of 45° just below a node. They are then placed in water.

Preparation of cuttings

Setting cuttings

When the cuttings are ready they are treated with a fungicide, such as *Captan* or *Kocide*. The basal cut of the stems is dipped in a **rooting hormone**, that is, a substance which hastens root development, and they are set immediately in the propagator. You will remember that some cuttings may be potted before they are placed in the propagator.

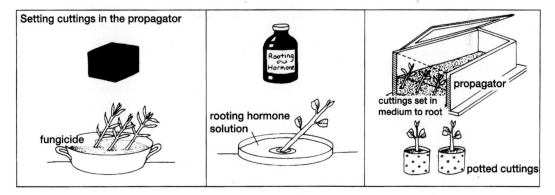

Setting cuttings in the propagator

fungicide

rooting hormone solution

propagator

cuttings set in medium to root

potted cuttings

Care of cuttings in the propagator

Cuttings placed in the propagator must be watered daily. Fallen leaves and cuttings which show wilting or fungal infection, such as black spot or browning, must be removed.

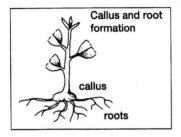

Callus and root formation

callus

roots

You should uproot a few cuttings at weekly intervals. Observe the length of time taken for **callus** formation, that is, the growth of new tissue, and for root development.

In order to get good root development, the propagator should be protected from drying winds. The light intensity must be reduced and the temperature and humidity in the propagating bins should be maintained at a high level.

Potting and hardening out rooted cuttings

When the cuttings have developed a number of roots, they are gently uprooted and potted. Your teacher will show you how to do this. The potted plants are kept in open bins in the propagator and watered regularly. After a period of 10 to 12 days, they are removed to a cool shady spot and then later exposed to full sunlight.

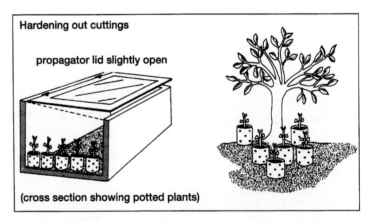

Hardening out cuttings

propagator lid slightly open

(cross section showing potted plants)

Propagation of plants by means of layering

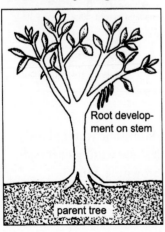

Root development on stem

parent tree

Some garden plants are propagated by means of **layering**. Do you know what a layer is? It is the development of roots on a stem which is still attached to the parent tree. The picture on the left will help you to understand this.

Consider the following questions:

1 Do all stems root readily?
2 Can stems be induced to form roots?
3 Under what conditions do layers set roots?

Layers may be done in several ways. In this lesson we will look at two methods that are in common use.

The simple layer

Take a soft stem from a coleus or a Spanish thyme plant and gently pull it down to the ground. Peg it down as shown in the following diagram and cover it with moist

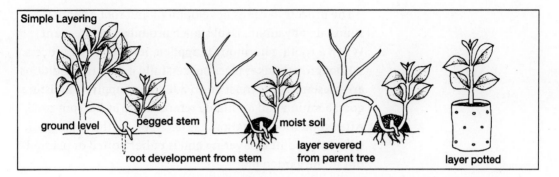

Simple Layering

ground level — pegged stem

root development from stem

moist soil

layer severed from parent tree

layer potted

soil to a depth of 5 cm. Keep the soil moist and look for root development after a period of three to four weeks.

When root growth has taken place, cut the stem from the parent plant. A week later dig out the new plant with its roots attached to the soil and either pot it or plant it directly in the garden plot. Keep the soil moist by watering.

Air layering

Some woody plants, such as shrubs and small trees, do not grow branches near to the ground. The branches of these plants are often stiff and difficult to bend. Such plants may be best propagated by means of air layering.

1 Study the pictures and illustrations in the figure below.
2 List the materials that are needed to air layer a plant.
3 List four steps in the process of air layering.
4 Put them in order of sequence.

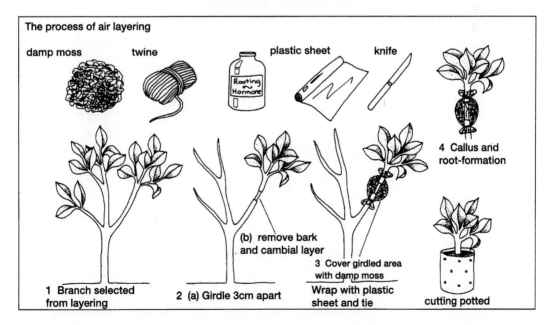

The process of air layering

damp moss   twine   plastic sheet   knife

Rooting Hormone

4 Callus and root-formation

(b) remove bark and cambial layer

3 Cover girdled area with damp moss
Wrap with plastic sheet and tie

1 Branch selected from layering

2 (a) Girdle 3cm apart

cutting potted

The process of callus development and root growth is stimulated by auxin, a substance produced by the plant. When a rooting hormone is applied, it hastens the process.

Root growth takes place successfully if certain conditions are present. There must be an adequate supply of moisture, good aeration and a suitable temperature at the root zone. After good root formation has taken place, the shoot is cut below the point of layering and is either potted or planted out in the garden plot.

Propagation by means of budding and grafting

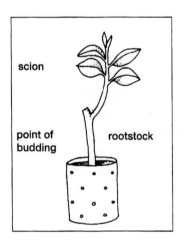

scion

point of budding

rootstock

Citrus, avocadoes and mangoes are often propagated by means of **budding and grafting**. In this method, the buds or the stem and leaves of one plant are induced to grow on the roots of another plant. This picture shows you a budded citrus plant. The part below the point of budding is known as the **rootstock** and the shoot which grows out of the bud is known as the **scion**.

In order to understand more about budding and grafting we need to consider the following questions:

1 Which types of plant can be budded and grafted?
2 How is budding and grafting done?
3 Why does a union take place between the rootstock and the scion?
4 What advantages does a farmer gain by the use of budded and grafted plants?

Plants suitable for budding and grafting

The following observations were made on the types of rootstock and scions used at a propagating centre:

Budded or grafted plant	Scion	Rootstock
Navel orange	Navel orange	*Cleopatra* mandarin
Lime	Lime	Lemon
Julie mango	*Julie* mango	Long mango (vert)
Pollock avocado	*Pollock* avocado	Common avocado
Pommecythere	Pommecythere	Hog-plum
Red rose	Red rose	Briar (wild rose)

From the observations above you will notice that budding and grafting can only take place between plants that are closely related to each other, that is, the rootstock and the scion must belong to the same family or species of plant.

How to bud a citrus plant

There are three major steps in the budding process.

1 The selection and preparation of budwood

Budwood is taken from a desirable parent tree and is usually selected from the stem before the last flush. The leaves are pruned by cutting their petioles as close as possible to the stem without damage to the buds. The prepared budwood is then wrapped and kept in a damp piece of muslin cloth until it is ready for use.

1 Selected stem to be used as budwood

2 Prepared wood

3 Budwood wrapped in damp muslin cloth

Preparation of budwood

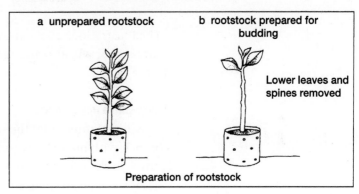

a unprepared rootstock

b rootstock prepared for budding

Lower leaves and spines removed

Preparation of rootstock

2 The preparation of rootstock

Rootstocks are grown from *Cleopatra* mandarin or lemon seeds which may be sown directly in the ground or in potting bags. Stocks are ready for budding when they are about 60–75 cm tall and about the thickness of a pencil. Only strong, healthy and vigorous stocks should be used.

3 The budding operation (⊥ or shield budding)

Budding must be done quickly and skilfully. An inverted 'T' cut is made on the rootstock at a height of 38–45 cm above the ground. A bud is removed from the budwood by means of a clean sharp cut and inserted in the rootstock by gently lifting the bark and pushing the bud upwards along the vertical cut. The bud is then wrapped with a **budding tape** made of ships-pitch and bees-wax or with a resinous plastic tape.

After a period of 10 days, the tape is unwrapped to a point below the bud. If the bud is still green it is likely to grow. The head of the rootstock is broken back and later removed completely when the inserted bud begins to shoot.

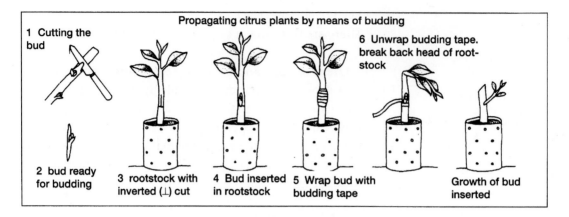

Propagating citrus plants by means of budding

1 Cutting the bud

2 bud ready for budding

3 rootstock with inverted (⊥) cut

4 Bud inserted in rootstock

5 Wrap bud with budding tape

6 Unwrap budding tape. break back head of root-stock

Growth of bud inserted

The illustrations above show you how citrus is budded. Your teacher will also arrange to have this process demonstrated to you.

How to graft a mango plant

You will remember that the scion used in a graft consists of a branch with many buds and leaves. The scion can be grafted on the rootstock in several ways. In this lesson we will look at side grafting, a method that is in popular use.

The side graft

In side grafting the scion is cut from the parent tree and then grafted on to the rootstock. The scion consists of a mature shoot that is about to set a new flush of growth. The leaves are removed by cutting their petioles as closely as possible to the stem whilst the cut at the base of the

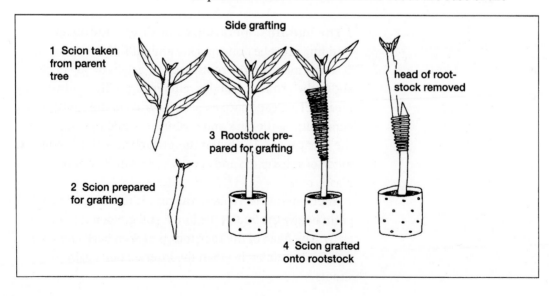

Side grafting

1 Scion taken from parent tree

2 Scion prepared for grafting

3 Rootstock prepared for grafting

4 Scion grafted onto rootstock

head of root-stock removed

scion must be long and slanted. A similar cut is made on the stem of the rootstock. The scion is then fitted on to the rootstock, bound firmly with raffia or twine and protected with budding tape.

The graft is inspected after 21 days. If the scion is still green it is likely to grow. The crown of the rootstock is now partially removed. When the crown grows out, the remaining head of the rootstock is completely cut back about 3–4 cm above the graft.

The union of the rootstock and the scion

A budded or grafted plant is produced when there is a successful union between the rootstock and the scion. Such a union takes place readily in plants that are closely related, and when the rootstock and the scion are of the same thickness and of the same stage of growth.

The budding and grafting operations must be done quickly and skilfully, so as to bring the cambial surfaces into quick and close contact. The best results are obtained when budding and grafting materials are clean and free from diseases and infection. Weather conditions must also be favourable, that is, it must not be too wet at grafting or budding time.

The advantages of budding and grafting

Observe a **well managed orchard** that is established with budded and grafted plants. Notice that the size and quality of fruits are similar to those of the parent tree from which the scion was taken. You will see also that the trees come into bearing earlier and they tend to spread and remain short. Such trees are not difficult to manage and their fruits are easily harvested.

Budded and grafted plants are often adapted to grow under varying climatic conditions and in different soil types. They may also be more resistant to diseases. As a result you get plants that are healthy and vigorous and which last longer than plants grown from seeds.

Summary

The stem cuttings of some plants will only set roots in a propagator, that is, a special bin filled with a rooting medium such as sand or fibre bast. To get good root development the propagator should be protected from drying winds. The

A well managed orchard

light intensity must be reduced and the temperature and humidity in the bin must be maintained at a high level.

Cuttings are selected from desirable parent trees and are usually taken early in the morning. They are prepared, treated with a fungicide and a rooting hormone and then set in the propagating bin. The bin is watered regularly. After a period of three to four weeks, root development takes place. The plants are then potted out and placed in a cool spot to grow.

In the process of layering, root development on the stem is induced while the plant is still attached to the parent tree. This may be done simply by pegging the stem down to the ground, covering with soil and kept moist. When root development takes place, the plant is cut, dug out and potted.

In woody plants (shrubs and small trees) air layering is practised. This involves the selection of a suitable branch, girdling and removing the bark and cambial tissues, applying a rooting hormone and enclosing with damp moss. Root development takes place in three to four weeks. The plant is then removed from the parent tree and potted out.

Some plants, such as citrus, avocadoes and mangoes, are best propagated by budding and grafting. The buds or the stem and leaves of one plant (called the scion) are induced to grow on the roots of another plant (called the rootstock). A good union of scion and rootstock takes place when the plants are closely related and the scion and the rootstock are of the same thickness and stage of growth.

In order to get good results, the budding and grafting operations must be done quickly and the cambial areas should be in close contact.

Budded or grafted plants produce fruits similar to those of the parent tree. They come into bearing earlier and the trees tend to spread out and remain short. This facilitates the easy management of trees and the harvesting of fruits.

Remember these

Budding and grafting	The bud or the stem with leaves from one plant is induced to grow on the root of another plant.
Budding tape	A special tape prepared for use in budding and grafting operations.
Budwood	A piece of stem from which buds are selected for budding.
Callus	The growth of new plant tissues at cut or injured surfaces.
Layering	The practice of inducing root development on a stem which is still attached to the parent tree.
Orchard	A plot of land cultivated with fruit trees.
Plant propagator	A device specially constructed to propagate plants from stem cuttings.
Rooting hormone	A chemical substance which stimulates root development.
Rootstock	The part of the plant which forms the root system in a budded or grafted plant.
Scion	The part of the plant which forms the shoot system in a budded or grafted plant.

Practical activities

1 Take 10 stem cuttings from the plants listed in the table below and set them to grow in your garden plots or in potting bags. Water them regularly and look for signs of growth by the end of the fourth or fifth week:

Now complete the observations in the table below.

Plant	Number of cuttings set	Number of cuttings grown
Cassava	10	
Sugar-cane	10	
Cocoa	10	
Guava	10	
Hibiscus	10	

   a Which stem cuttings grow quite readily by simply placing them in the soil?

   b Which stem cutting should be set in a plant propagator for root development?

2 Select and prepare 10 stem cuttings from croton or hibiscus plants. Set them in your school propagator and water regularly. Observe for root development.

  a Did the cuttings set roots?

  b How long did they take to set roots?

3 Select branches from the plants listed in the table below. Perform air layering on them and then complete the rest of the observations in the table.

Plant	Date of layering	Date of root set	Date of potting out	Did the plant grow or die?
Croton				
Hibiscus				
Aralia				
Guava				
Rose				
Ixora				

  a Did all the layers set roots?

  b Which layers took a shorter time to set roots?

  c Which layers took a longer time to set roots?

  d What conclusion can you make from these observations?

4 Investigate more about budding and grafting and then complete this table:

Type of plant	Scion	Rootstock
Citrus	Grapefruit	
	Valencia orange	
	Limes	
Avocado	Pollock	
	Lula	
Mango	Julie	
	Graham	

State a major factor that should be considered in the selection of rootstock in relation to the scion.

Do these test exercises

1 **Select the best answer from the choices given.**

   a **A plant propagator is a special device for propagating plants from**

   A seeds.

   B rhizomes.

   C stem cuttings.

   D leaf cuttings.

   b **Which of these conditions is *not* desirable in a plant propagator**

   A high temperature.

   B high humidity.

   C low light intensity.

   D exposure to dry winds.

   c **The process of inducing root development on a stem which is still attached to the parent tree is described as**

   A propagating

   B layering

   C budding

   D grafting

   d **Which of these plants is generally propagated by grafting?**

   A Navel orange.

   B Lime.

   C Julie mango.

   D Avocado.

   e **A successful union of rootstock and scion takes place when they are**

   (i) closely related.

   (ii) of the same thickness.

   (iii) of the same stage of growth.

   In the statements above

   A only (i) is correct.

   B only (i) and (ii) are correct.

   C only (ii) and (iii) are correct.

   D (i), (ii) and (iii) are all correct.

2 **Explain the following in your own words:**

   a Rooting hormone.

   b Callus formation.

   c Rooting medium.

   d Parent trees with desirable characteristics.

   e A union between rootstock and scion.

3 **Tell why:**

   a Budding and grafting operations must be done quickly and neatly.

   b Budding is done at a height of 38–45 cm above the ground.

   c Cuttings should be kept in a container with water.

   d The scion from a Julie mango tree would not form a union with a citrus rootstock.

4 **Say how you would:**

   a Air layer a rose plant.

   b Select budwood from a citrus tree.

   c Prevent the development and spread of fungal diseases in a plant propagator.

   d Prepare budding tape at home.

5 **Say how the following differ from each other:**

   a Simple layering and air layering.

   b Rootstock and scion.

   c Budding and grafting.

6 **Make a list of the materials and apparatus required for budding a citrus plant. Say how these materials are used in the process of budding.**

7 **A farmer is advised to establish an orchard with budded and grafted plants. Write a short paragraph saying why this is advisable.**

2 The cultivation of vegetable fruit crops

Lesson objectives

In this lesson you are going to learn about the cultivation of vegetable fruit crops. At the end of the lesson you should be able to:

1 Describe the cultivation practices of a vegetable fruit crop.

2 Cultivate sweet-peppers and cucumbers

3 Select suitable fertilisers for vegetable fruit crops at different stages of growth

In Books One and Two you learnt how to cultivate corn and vegetable crops such as tomatoes, beans, lettuce and carrots. In this lesson you are going to learn about the cultivation of sweet-peppers and cucumbers.

Sweet-peppers

Sweet-pepper crop

Mrs Roma is fond of sweet-peppers. She cultivates them in her home garden throughout the year. Sweet peppers can tolerate a wide variety of climatic conditions, and they grow quite well on a wide range of soil types.

Varieties

Several **varieties** of sweet-pepper are grown in the Caribbean. The chief ones are the *Canape* (left), the *Bullnose* and the *Keystone Resistant Giant*. Some **hybrid** types (crosses between two species) are also cultivated. However, Mrs

The Canape variety of sweet-pepper

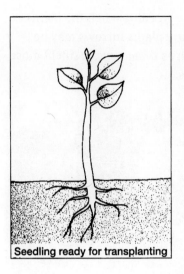
Seedling ready for transplanting

Roma prefers the *Bullnose*. The plants grow vigorously and come into bearing 6 to 8 weeks after planting. The fruits are large and **succulent**.

Planting material

Seeds are sown in seed-boxes or on seed-beds. When the seedlings are about 10–15 cm tall, they are lifted with soil attached to their roots and **transplanted** to the garden plots.

Find out why Mrs Roma:
1 Does not plant seeds directly in the garden plots.
2 Lifts seedlings with soil attached to their roots.

Soil and land preparation

Sweet-peppers grow on soils which vary from sandy loams to light clays. However, they thrive best on a deep loamy soil that is well drained and in which there are large quantities of compost or pen manure.

Planting and spacing

Planting distances vary according to the soil type. On rich loamy soils the plants are placed in rows 60–75 cm apart and a distance of 50–60 cm between plants in the rows.

On poorer soils these distances may be reduced. By so doing the plant population is increased and as a result the yield of crop is also increased.

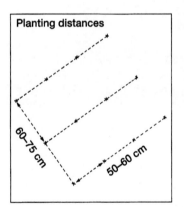
Planting distances
60–75 cm
50–60 cm

Watering

Mrs Roma waters her plants immediately after transplanting. In the dry season she applies a grass **mulch** on the soil and irrigates with an overhead sprinkler.

Do you know how a grass mulch helps the soil? It reduces the loss of soil moisture by **evaporation** and keeps the soil cool. It also prevents competition by weeds by depressing their growth. On decomposition, it adds organic matter to the soil. You will remember that organic matter is rich in nutrients. It improves soil structure and increases the water holding capacity of the soil.

Weed control

Weeds are harmful to the plants in their early stages of growth. They overcrowd the cultivated plants and rob them of light, water and nutrient supplies.

Weeds are best controlled by weeding when the plants are young. In fields with mature plants furrows may be sprayed with a weedicide such as *Gramoxone*. A shield must be used to prevent spray drifts.

A shield prevents spray drift during weedicide application

Moulding and staking

Moulding is necessary to keep water from the roots of the plants. When in full bearing, the plants become heavy and tend to fall to the ground. **Staking** keeps them upright, reduces shaking and prevents the fruits from touching the ground.

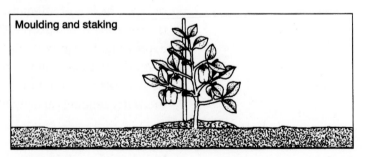

Moulding and staking

Fertiliser treatment

A mixed fertiliser, rich in phosphate, is applied to the soil at planting time. Three weeks later, each sweet-pepper plant is given 30–40 g of sulphate of ammonia as a surface dressing. In the absence of sulphate of ammonia, 15–20 g of urea may be used instead.

When flowering begins, the plant receives 40–55 g of N.P.K. high in potash. This treatment is repeated every 2 to 3 weeks.

In the early stages of growth, phosphate helps root development and sulphate of ammonia provides nitrogen for vegetative growth. Later on, potash is essential in developing flowers and fruits.

Pest and disease control

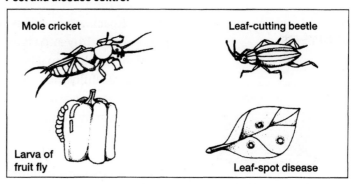

Sweet-peppers are attacked by such pests as mole crickets, leaf-cutting beetles, the larvae of fruit flies and nematodes. Amongst the diseases leaf-spot and virus infections are prevalent. This table shows you how Mrs Roma controls these pests and diseases.

Pests and diseases	Control measures
Mole crickets	Spray soil with an insecticide, e.g. *Diazinon* or *Primicid*.
Fruit flies and leaf-cutting beetles	Spray plants with *Malathion*
Nematodes	Treat the soil with a nematicide, e.g. *Furadan* or *Formaldehyde*, a few weeks prior to planting.
Leaf-spots	Spray plant with a copper fungicide, e.g. *Kocide*
Virus infection	Plant disease free seeds; rotate crops; remove and burn infected plants

Harvesting

Fruits are harvested when they are in the matured green stage. They should be picked gently as sweet-pepper branches break quite easily. On heavily laden trees, some fruits should be removed even if they are immature.

Try to find out how heavy bearing may be damaging to a plant.

Sweet-pepper as a food

Sweet-peppers have a high content of vitamins A and C. Small amounts of calcium and iron are also present. How does Mrs Roma utilise her sweet-peppers?

1 Does she use them in stews, soups and salads?
2 Does she **pickle** and store them for future use?

Cucumbers

Fruits of the cucumber

Farmer Roach grows cucumber in his market garden. His plants are healthy and vigorous and they bear large fruits. Cucumbers belong to a family of plants called **cucurbits**. Observe carefully their stems, leaves, flowers and fruits, and then name *two* other plants that you think belong to the same family group. Give reasons for your selection.

Varieties

The chief types of cucumber found in the Caribbean are the *Chipper*, the *Regal*, the *Calypso* and the *Burpee Hybrid*. Farmer Roach cultivates the first two types as these grow vigorously and bear heavily.

Cucumber

Planting material

Cucumbers are propagated by seeds which are obtained from garden shops or collected from healthy mature ripe fruits. Seeds kept in proper storage show good viability up to a period of 4 to 6 months.

Soil and land preparation

Cucumbers grow well on loams and light clays that are not acid. Farmer Roach ensures that his soil is dug deeply and is well drained. He incorporates liberal quantities of pen or compost manures as well as mixed fertilisers (10.15.10) in the soil at preparation time.

Planting and spacing

Seeds are sown directly in the garden plots. They are placed in rows 120 cm apart and 60–75 cm between the plants in the rows.

   Two or three times as many seeds are planted in the holes as the number of plants that are required. This allows for wilting which frequently occurs, and for **thinning out**. This is a process in which Farmer Roach removes the weak seedlings and leaves about three healthy ones to the stool.

Aftercare

Watering

Watering is necessary in the dry season. This is best done by means of overhead sprinkler irrigation or by channel irrigation.

Weed control

Farmer Roach begins weed control just before the cucumbers are ready to vine.

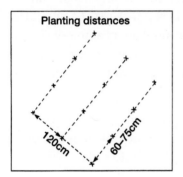

Planting distances
120cm
60–75cm

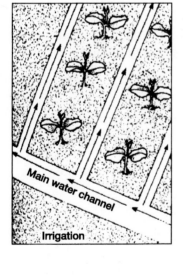

Main water channel
Irrigation

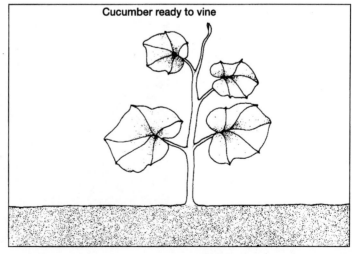

Cucumber ready to vine

He hand picks the weeds around the plants to a distance of 20–30 cm from the roots and then sprays the furrows with *Gramoxone*. He sprays early in the morning when it is not very windy and uses a spray shield to protect the crop from spray drifts.

Fertiliser treatment

Each cucumber stool is treated with a surface dressing of 56–70 g of sulphate of ammonia at intervals of 14 to 21 days until flowering time. After this, treatments of a mixed fertiliser high in potash, such as N.P.K. 10.10.17, should be made. You will remember that sulphate of ammonia supplies nitrogen which promotes vegetative growth and potash helps in the development of flowers and fruits.

Pest and disease control

Farmer Roach observes that his cucumbers are attacked by fruit-flies and aphids. The larvae of the fruit-flies burrow into the fruits whilst aphids suck the juices of the young leaves and shoots. The farmer sprays regularly with *Malathion* for effective control.

Among the fungal diseases present are downy and powdery mildews. The former appear as white fungal threads and the latter as a white film on the stems and leaves. These are controlled with copper and sulphur fungicides respectively.

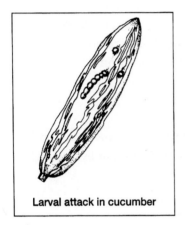

Larval attack in cucumber

Harvest and yield

The plant comes into bearing about 8 weeks after planting. Farmer Roach harvests the fruits every week and picks

Farmers and their crops of cucumbers

them before they reach the full mature stage. Each plant gives a yield of 10 to 12 fruits.

The cucumber as a food

Cucumbers contain small quantities of calcium, iron and vitamin C. The fruits are eaten raw or used in salads. They are also pickled and stored for future use. In some countries the stem and leaves are used as a spinach or bhaji.

Summary

Sweet-peppers and cucumbers are two vegetable fruit crops commonly grown in home gardens.

Sweet-peppers can be cultivated under a variety of climatic conditions and on a wide range of soil types. However, they thrive best in a well drained loamy soil rich in organic matter.

Among the many varieties of sweet-peppers the *Canape* and the *Bullnose* are the most popular varieties in cultivation. Seedlings are prepared in a nursery, and when they are 10–15 cm tall they are transplanted into the garden plots in rows at a distance of 60–75 cm apart and a distance of 50–60 cm between plants in the rows. Further care and management of the crop involves watering, weed control, moulding and staking, pest and disease control and the application of fertilisers.

The plants come into bearing at 6 to 8 weeks after planting. The fruits are large and succulent and are a good source of vitamins A and C.

Cucumbers belong to a family of plants called cucurbits. Like sweet-peppers, cucumbers can grow under a variety of climatic conditions and on a wide range of soil types. The soil must be tilled, well drained and treated with liberal amounts of pen manure. The inclusion of a mixed fertiliser rich in phosphates is also essential for root development in the early stages of growth.

There are several varieties of cucumber, but the most popular ones are the *Regal* and the *Chipper*. The seeds are planted directly in the field plots in rows 120 cm apart and 60–75 cm between the plants in the rows. After germination, the seedlings are gradually thinned out to 2 or 3 plants per stool. The plants are watered regularly and kept free from weeds. Other management practices include the application of fertilisers and the use of sprays to control pests and diseases.

The plant comes into bearing about 8 weeks after planting. Fruits are usually harvested just before the fully mature stage and are used as salads or pickled and stored for future use.

Remember these

Evaporation	Loss of moisture by drying winds.
Hybrid	The plant arising from the cross between two species.
Moulding	The act of pulling soil around the stem and roots of a plant.
Mulch	A surface dressing of the soil preferably with organic materials.
Pickle	The preservation of fruits or vegetables in brine or vinegar.
Staking	A stake placed near a plant for support.
Succulent	Soft and juicy.
Thinning out	Reducing the number of seedlings in a stool.
Transplanted	Seedlings taken from a nursery and planted out into a garden plot.
Varieties	Groups of plants differing in some common qualities from the rest of the class to which they belong.

Practical activities

1 Select a plot in your school garden for planting cucumbers. Measure and stake the planting distances of 120 cm between rows and 75 cm between plants in the rows.

Make a sketch or drawing of the exercise you completed.

2 Your teacher will provide specimens of sulphate of ammonia, urea, super-phosphate and potash. Observe them carefully and then complete the table below. A sample is done for you.

Observations	Fertilisers			
	Sulphate of ammonia	Urea	Super-phosphate	Potash
What is its colour?	White			
Is it fine grained, coarse grained or granular?	Coarse grained			
Is it crystalline or non-crystalline?	Crystalline			

Give a description of the physical nature of these fertilisers. For example, sulphate of ammonia is a white coarse grained crystalline substance.

Do these test exercises

1 **Consider these statements carefully. State whether they are *true* or *false*.**

 a Succulent fruits are hard and dry.

 b Close planting distances are recommended on poor soil types.

 c The main purpose of a surface mulch in the dry season is to conserve soil moisture.

 d Organic matter is a poor source of nutrient.

 e Pickling is a method of preserving fruits and vegetables.

2 **Select the best answer from the choices given.**

 a The *Bullnose* is a variety of

 A ochro.

 B sweet-pepper.

 C cabbage.

 D cucumber.

 b **Sweet-pepper thrives best on**

 A sand.

 B clay.

 C loam.

 D silt.

 c **An example of a fungicide is**

 A *Kocide.*

 B *Furadan.*

 C *Diazinon.*

 D *Malathion.*

 d **Some sweet-pepper plants are fertilised with sulphate of ammonia. This treatment is intended to promote**

 A root development.

 B vegetative growth.

 C resistance to diseases.

 D flowering and fruiting.

 e **Which fertiliser is best suited for cucumbers in the flowering and fruiting stage?**

 A Urea.

 B Sulphate of ammonia.

 C Super-phosphate.

 D Potash.

3 **Tell why:**

 a Sweet-peppers in heavy

bearing should be staked.

 b Plants that are sown thickly should be thinned out.

 c Cucumbers should be harvested before they reach the fully mature stage.

4 **Say how the following garden operations are important in the production of sweet-peppers or cucumbers.**

 a Soil-drainage.

 b The application of pen or compost manures to the soil.

 c The use of grass mulches.

 d Irrigation practices.

 e The control of weeds.

5 **Name suitable fertilisers which are good for vegetable fruit crops at each of the following stages of plant growth:**

 a At planting time.

 b Two weeks after planting.

 c When flower and fruit-set begin.

Give reasons for the fertilisers you have selected.

3

Crops of economic importance – sugar cane

Lesson objectives

In this lesson you are going to learn about sugar-cane. On completing this lesson you should be able to:

1 Explain the term economic crop.

2 Describe the origin and spread of sugar-cane to the Caribbean.

3 List the three main groups of sugar-cane and state their characteristic features.

4 Give a simple description of the structure of the sugar-cane plant.

5 State the conditions essential for the successful growth of sugar-cane.

6 Describe the cultivation practices of sugar-cane.

7 List the manufactured products derived from sugar-cane.

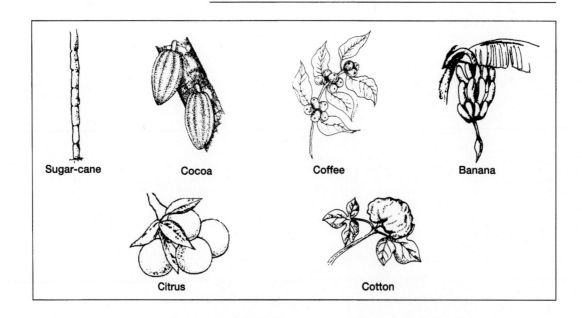

Sugar-cane   Cocoa   Coffee   Banana

Citrus   Cotton

The picture on page 24 show you some field crops of economic importance. These crops are grown in large plantations mainly for export so as to earn foreign exchange. Sugar-cane is grown throughout the tropics and in many sub-tropical countries. It is one of the chief economic crops in the Caribbean and in the surrounding mainland countries of Mexico, Central America, Venezuela and Guyana.

The diagram below tells you about the origin and spread of sugar-cane. It is believed that sugar-cane originated in the island of New Guinea and was later transplanted in India and Southern China where the first sugar-cane plantations were found. The cultivation of sugar-cane continued to spread to the Middle East from where it was taken by the Arabs to Egypt, Morocco, Spain, and the Mediterranean island of Sicily.

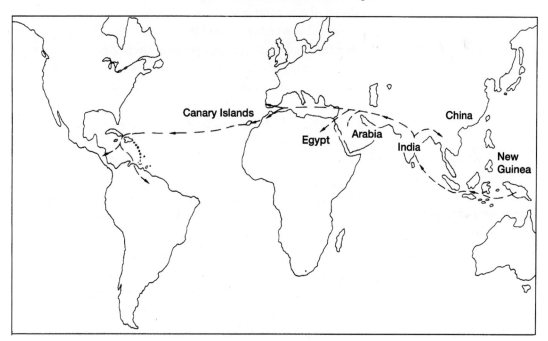

In the fifteenth century sugar-cane was introduced into the Canary Islands and from there it was brought by the Spaniards to the Caribbean and Latin American countries.

Varieties

There are many varieties of sugar-cane.

Thick or noble canes

The chief cane in the group is the *Bourbon*. The stem is thick, soft, juicy and barrel-shaped. It has a high sucrose

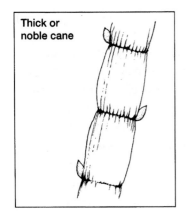

Thick or noble cane

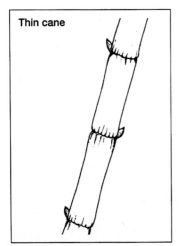

Thin cane

content (sugar content), and tends to flourish well under tropical conditions. However, this cane has poor **tillering** qualities and it is very susceptible to diseases. At present it is chiefly grown in home gardens as cane for chewing.

Thin canes

These canes have thin, slender stems with long internodes. They are generally hard and fibrous and only contain a small amount of juice with poor sucrose content. However, thin canes are very vigorous, disease resistant, and they tiller freely. These latter characteristics make thin canes very desirable and important in sugar-cane breeding programmes.

Commercial hybrids

Most of our commercial canes are hybrids produced from crosses between thick and thin canes. As a result these commercial varieties are noted for their vigour, disease resistance, high yields and high sucrose content. Two outstanding hybrid types in the Caribbean are the B.37161 and B.41227. These varieties were bred in Barbados. In your country there may be other hybrid varieties in commercial production.

Structure of the sugar-cane plant

Like corn and rice, the sugar-cane belongs to the family of plants called Gramineae that is, the grass family.

Observe a stool of sugar-cane carefully. You will notice that the plant is fibrous rooted and the stem is solid with nodes and internodes. At each node, there is a bud or eye and a band of **root initials** from which adventitious roots develop. The soft pith, that is the tissue under the **epidermis** is sweet and juicy.

The leaf is long, narrow and pointed. The leaf base forms a sheath around the stem. At the top of the plant, the **arrow** (the inflorescence) appear.

Study the drawings on page 27. They will help you to recognise the structural features of the sugar-cane plant.

Conditions for growth

Sugar-cane grows best on rich porous soils. However, it adapts itself to almost all types of soil. The most suitable climate is one with high temperatures, abundant rainfall and

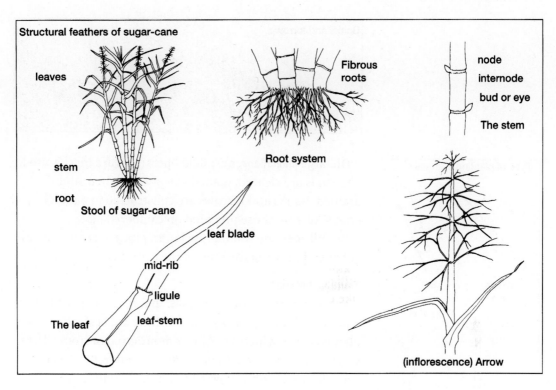

plenty of sunlight. A temperature range of 29°C to 32°C is quite satisfactory whilst an annual rainfall of 150 cm is adequate. Long dry spells with plenty of sunlight are desirable at reaping time. These conditions promote sucrose development in the sugar-cane and facilitate harvesting.

Soil and land preparation

You will remember that sugar-cane adapts itself to all types of soil. However, on heavy clays deep ploughing and good drainage are absolutely essential.

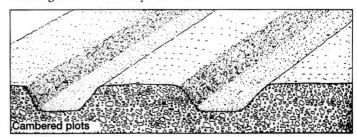

On small estates where little or no mechanisation is used the land is generally ploughed and prepared into **cambered** plots. Banks and furrows are opened with the ridges 1–2 m apart and the furrows 15–45 cm deep, from the surface of the ground to the bottom of the furrows.

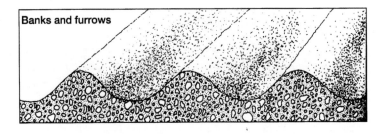
Banks and furrows

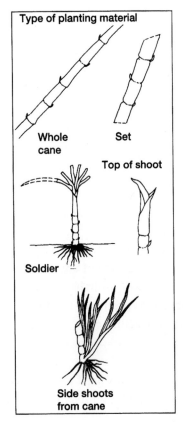
Type of planting material

Whole cane

Set

Top of shoot

Soldier

Side shoots from cane

On large **plantations** most field operations are mechanised. The lands are cleared, graded, deeply ploughed, and drained. Banks and furrows are constructed in parallel lines similar to those prepared on cambered plots.

On hillsides and undulating lands, ploughing and ridging are done following the lines of the contours.

Planting material

Planting materials consist of **setts**, that is, cuttings with 2 or 3 nodes, whole canes or soldiers. These are best taken from planted canes which are 8 to 12 months old or from **ratoons** which are 6 to 8 months old. Setts are generally used by small farmers whilst large estates and plantations use whole canes. Soldiers are not very desirable and should only be used as a last resort. All planting materials must be free from pests and diseases. It is advisable to treat them with a disinfectant before they are planted.

Planting and spacing

Cuttings are laid horizontally in the furrows 20–50 cm apart and covered to a depth of 5–6 cm on heavy soils or to a depth of 10 cm on lighter soils.

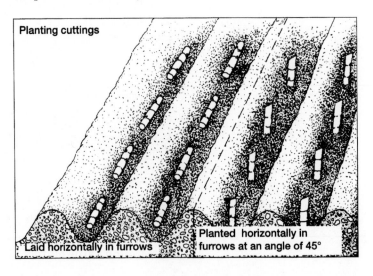
Planting cuttings

Laid horizontally in furrows

Planted horizontally in furrows at an angle of 45°

Many farmers prefer to plant cuttings horizontally at an angle of 45° as this encourages quick tillering and rapid stool development.

Whole canes used for planting are laid in the furrows with an overlapping of the top end of one cane and the base end of another. Sometimes it is necessary to cut the canes so as to settle them in the furrows. The canes are then covered with soil as is done with cuttings. As the shoots grow up, the banks are gradually broken to fill up the furrows.

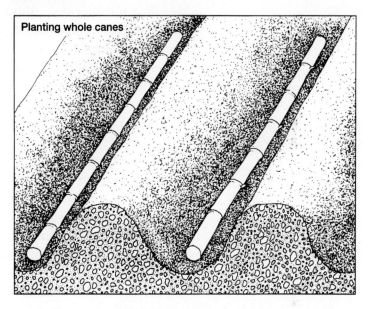

Planting whole canes

Sugar-cane buds germinate best under moist conditions. Consequently, the best time to plant is in the early wet season, or 4 to 6 weeks earlier if irrigation is available.

Care and management
Irrigation
Sugar-cane needs an abundant supply of water during its growing season. A shortage of water may lead to very poor harvests. Under wet tropical conditions irrigation may only be necessary during periods of drought. This is done either by sprinkler irrigation at planting time or by the use of flood or furrow irrigation in growing canes.

Weed control
Weeds are most harmful to sugar-cane in their early stages of growth. Weeds may be controlled mechanically by

Suitable equipment for spraying sugar-cane

weeding and inter-row cultivation, or chemically by the use of weedicides such as *2,4-D, Gramoxone, Atrazine* or *Asulox* with *Actril D*. In your country there may be other types of weedicides in common use.

It is important to remember that weedicides should be carefully selected and used according to the manufacturer's instructions.

Fertiliser applications

Sugar-cane grows vigorously and extracts large quantities of nutrient elements from the soil. Under intense cultivation the soil needs to be properly fertilised.

The chief nutrient elements required by the plant are nitrogen, phosphorus and potash. These are supplied as fertilisers and the quantities to be applied are determined from soil and foliar analyses and from fertiliser trials.

The table below tells you more about the sources and importance of these major nutrient elements in sugar-cane production.

Nutrient element	Fertiliser source	Importance
Nitrogen	a Urea b Sulphate of ammonia	It promotes vegetative growth and is important in the early stages of plant growth and for ratoons soon after harvesting.
Phosphorus	Superphosphates (18%)	Aids root development and early tillering. Has favourable effect on height and thickness of stem and on juice quality.
Potash	Muriate of potash	Essential for the synthesis of carbohydrates and the production of sucrose.

Application of lime

You will remember that lime is a rich source of calcium. This element is not only an essential plant nutrient but it also assists in the formation of sugar in the plant. Lime improves the physical condition of the soil and removes soil acidity which builds up as a result of the constant use of nitrogenous fertilisers such as sulphate of ammonia and urea. An application of lime every 2 or 3 years is necessary for healthy sugar-cane growth and good yields.

Pest and disease control

Let us consider some of the sugar-cane pests and diseases that are prevalent in the Caribbean and in other tropical countries.

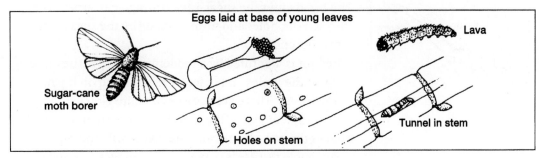

Eggs laid at base of young leaves

Lava

Sugar-cane moth borer

Tunnel in stem

Holes on stem

The sugar-cane moth borer

Have you seen holes and tunnels in the stems and joints of the sugar-cane? You may have noticed too, that the stems dry out and are easily broken by the wind. This damage is done by the sugar-cane borer.

The moth deposits its eggs in clusters on the leaves. Six to 7 days later the caterpillars hatch and enter the stem by way of the leaf shoot or by boring into the stem under the leaf sheath. About 6 weeks later the larvae pupate within the cane and the moth emerges.

The moth-borer is readily controlled by spraying the sugar-cane with an insecticide. Farmers must also ensure that their planting materials are free from moth-borer attacks.

Mealybugs and aphids

Mealybugs and aphids are sucking insects. They suck the juices of the plant and contaminate the leaves and stem with **honey dew** (sugary excretions) upon which the sooty mould (a fungus) thrives.

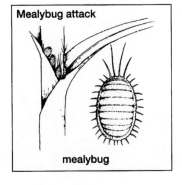

Mealybug attack

mealybug

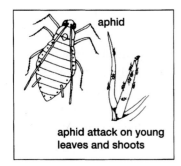

aphid

aphid attack on young leaves and shoots

Mealybug attacks produce red discolouration on the leaf sheaths near the nodes. They also lower the resistance of the plant to fungal infection. Aphids, however, cluster on the under surface of the leaves and in the young shoots. They are potential vectors of virus diseases.

Mealybugs and aphids are generally spread by infected planting materials or by ants with which they are in close association. The chief control methods are to ensure that all planting materials are free from mealybugs and aphids and to spray the cultivated fields periodically with an insecticide such as *Malathion*.

Red rot and pineapple disease

Red rot and pineapple disease are both fungal infections. The fungi enter the sugar-cane through cut surfaces or through the holes and tunnels made by the sugar-cane moth-borer.

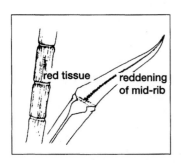

red tissue

reddening of mid-rib

Red rot is identified by a reddening of the tissues especially at the nodes and vascular regions and on the mid-rib of the leaves. There are occasional white blotches in the pith at right angles to the long axis of the stem. In severe attacks the pith shrinks and the leaves wilt and die.

Pineapple disease is prevalent in cool weather and on moist soils. The infected plants become reddish brown, brown, and eventually black. The presence of a pineapple odour is also detectable at the points of infection.

Red rot and pineapple disease are usually controlled by planting healthy materials that are treated with a fungicide. Spraying against the moth-borer also helps to reduce the incidence of these diseases.

Harvesting, processing and utilisation

Cutting sugar-cane mechanically by hand

Sugar-cane is harvested in the dry season when there is an abundance of sunshine and little or no rainfall. Under such conditions, the sucrose content of the sugar-cane is at its best.

Some farmers burn their canes before harvesting, many of them do not. However, all canes are either harvested mechanically by hand or by harvesting machines (see page 73) and are then transported to the factory where they are weighed and crushed. The juice is extracted, clarified and processed to give sugar and molasses. Do you know that these two products contain large quantities of carbohydrates and small amounts of proteins, minerals, and vitamin B?

Study this chart and it will give you an idea of the various products that are obtained from the sugar industry and how these products re utilised.

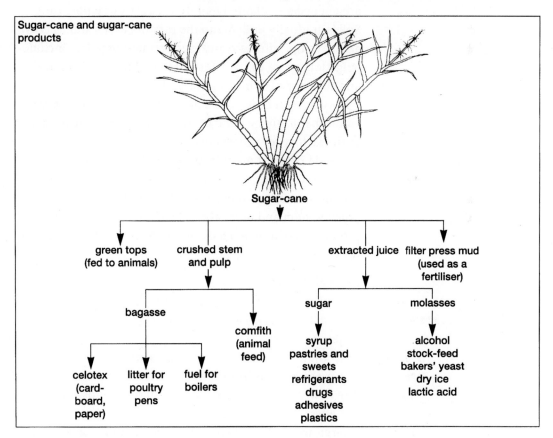

Sugar-cane and sugar-cane products

Summary

Sugar-cane is one of the chief economic crops grown in the tropics. It is believed that sugar-cane was originated in New Guinea and gradually found its way to the Canary

Islands from where it was brought by the Spaniards to the Caribbean and Latin American countries.

The crop can be grown under a wide range of climatic conditions and on a variety of soil types.

Sugar-cane is grouped as thick or noble canes, thin canes and commercial hybrids. In commercial plantations, hybrids are generally used as these canes are high yielding, rich in sucrose and resistant to diseases. The hybrids B.37161 and B.41227 are popularly used.

The crop grows best on porous soils. A temperature range of 29°C to 32°C is quite satisfactory and an annual rainfall of 150 cm is adequate. Long dry spells with plenty of sunlight are desirable at reaping time.

The land should be deeply ploughed and well drained. On heavy clays cambered plots are recommended. Furrows are opened and planted mainly with setts or whole cane. Soil is gradually pulled into the furrows as the shoots grow and develop. Aftercare and management practices include irrigation, weed control, fertiliser and lime applications and the control of insect pests and diseases.

Harvesting is done in the dry season. The crop is harvested mechanically by hand or by machines and transported to the factory for processing.

A wide range of manufactured products are obtained from the sugar-cane. From the extracted juice the main products are sugar, molasses and alcohol whilst the crushed stem and pulp, also called bagasse, is used in the production of animal feeds and in the manufacture of celotex cardboard and paper.

Remember these

Arrow	The inflorescence of the sugar-cane plant.
Cambered plots	Plots that are raised at the middle and gently sloping at the edges.
Epidermis	The outer tissue or covering of the plant.
Honey dew	Sugary excretions from aphids and mealybugs.
Hybrids	The new variety produced as a result of the crossing of two varieties.
Plantation	A large area of land under cultivation with a single crop.
Ratoons	The sugar-cane crops which follow after the crop of the first planting is harvested.
Root initials	Points on the nodes of the sugar-cane stem at which adventitious roots develop.

Setts	Pieces of sugar-cane stem consisting of two or three nodes used as planting material.
Tillering	The act of producing side shoots from the base of a plant especially in the grass family.

Practical activities

1 Observe a stool of sugar-cane. Make a labelled drawing showing the roots, the stems, the leaves and the arrows.

2 Collect the full length of a mature sugar-cane plant and measure the lengths of:
   a The last three internodes at the root end of the stem.
   b The last three internodes at the top end of the stem.
   c The three internodes at the middle of the stem.
   Comment on your observations.

3 Prepare a sett cutting from the sugar-cane stem and set it in a potting bag filled with garden soil. Place the potted cutting in a sheltered spot and water daily. Observe for root and shoot development.
   From what part of the cutting did
   a the root develop?
   b the shoot develop?

4 Collect and label the following:
   a Three manufactured products from the extracted juice of the sugar-cane.
   b Two products from the crushed stem and pulp.
   c Select one product from each of the groups (a) and (b) and state its uses.

Do these test exercises

1 Select the best answer from the choices given.

a It is believed that sugar-cane originated in
A India.
B New Guinea.
C Australia.
D Canary Islands.

b Sugar-cane was brought to the Caribbean by the
A French.
B Dutch.
C Spaniards.
D English.

c Sugar-cane thrives well on porous soil because the soil
A is rich in nutrient supplies.
B drains readily and is well aerated.
C has a high content of organic matter.
D is free from pests and diseases.

d A farmer indicated that the land must be ploughed deeply and well drained in order to grow a crop of sugar-cane. The soil type is probably
A a rich loam.
B a sandy loam.
C a light clay.
D a heavy clay.

e Hybrids of noble cane and thin cane are used in commercial sugar cane production. These hybrids are
(i) vigorous and disease resistant.
(ii) high yielding.
(iii) high in sucrose content.

Which of these statements is true about hybrid sugar-cane?
A (i) only.
B (i) and (ii) only.
C (ii) and (iii) only.
D (i), (ii) and (iii) are all true.

2 Explain in your own words:
a Ratoons.
b Tillering.
c Commercial varieties.

3 Tell why:
a Thin canes are desirable in breeding programmes.
b It is best to plant sugar-cane in the early part of the wet season.
c Ploughing and ridging must be done on the contours on hillsides.

4 Say how you would recognise and control the following insect pests in sugar-cane.
a Moth borer attack.
b Aphids and mealybug infestations.

5 State the importance of each of the following fertilisers in sugar-cane production:
a Urea.
b Superphosphate.
c Muriate of Potash.

6 Write a short description of the structure of the sugar-cane plant. Use the following heads as guides.
a Root.
b Stem.
c Leaf.
d Flower.

4 Pest and disease control in crops

Lesson objectives

Pest and disease attacks are often responsible for the reduction in yield and quality of crops. In this lesson you are going to learn about the control of pests and diseases in crops. On completing this lesson you should be able to:

1 Explain how pests and diseases in crops affect a farmer's income.

2 Give examples of pests and diseases of crops.

3 State the effects of pest and disease attacks on crops.

4 State the main methods of controlling pests, and diseases in crops.

5 Give a simple classification of (a) weedicides and (b) insecticides according to their mode of action.

6 Give examples of (a) mechanical methods, and (b) cultural methods of pest and disease control.

7 State some disadvantages and harmful effects associated with the use of chemicals in controlling pests and diseases.

8 State the safety measures that should be taken when using agricultural chemicals in the control of pests and diseases.

9 Explain the concepts of (a) biological control and (b) integrated pest management.

10 State the advantages to be gained by using the integrated pest management approach in controlling pests and diseases in crops.

In Book One we learnt that some of the biotic elements of the environment are useful in agriculture while others are harmful. These harmful elements or organisms are the ones that attack our crops either as pests or diseases.

Identify the following organisms and state how they are useful or harmful in agriculture.

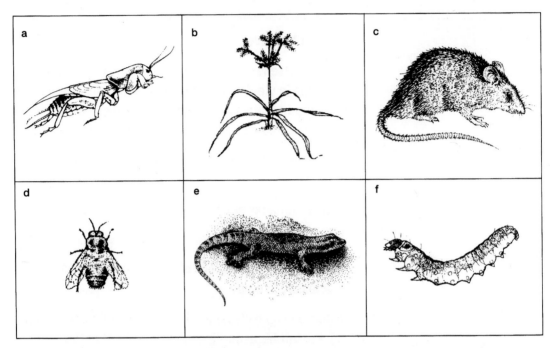

Pest and disease control is important in crop production. Consider these two questions carefully:

1 How do attacks from pests and diseases affect crop yield and crop quality?

2 What is the effect of crop yield and crop quality on a farmer's income?

When pests and diseases attack crops the yield and quality of produce is reduced. As a result, a farmer's income is also reduced.

Pests and diseases of crops

In our studies of vegetable and field crop production, we considered some of the pests and diseases which attack crops. The two tables on page 39 list some pests and diseases with examples and their effects on crops. Study them carefully.

Pests	Examples	Effect on crop
Weed	Fowlfoot grass, Nut grass, Bahama grass, Water grass, Railway Daisy, Broom weed, Sensitive plant.	1 Weeds compete with cultivated plants for soil water, nutrient supplies, air and light. 2 They harbour animals and insects that are harmful to crops.
Insect	Bachacs, aphids, whiteflies, mole-cricket, flea beetle, sugar-cane borer, scale insects, locust, leaf miners, caterpillars, mites, lacewing bug.	1 Insects cut, bite, chew, puncture and tunnel the leaves of plants. They also attack stem and root tubers 2 They suck the juices or sap of plants. They are also vectors of diseases. 3 Damage to leaves reduces leaf surface area. Photosynthesis is affected and ultimately crop yield and crop quality is reduced. 4 Secondary infection may set in causing rot and decay.
Animal	1 Wild animals, e.g. squirrel, agouti opossum. 2 Birds eg. Jackdaw, corn bird. 3 Rodents e.g. rats, mice.	Animals destroy fruits, grains and root tubers.
Plant parasite	1 Love Vine (total parasite, lacks chlorophyll). 2 Mistletoe (semi-parasite possesses leaves with chlorophyll).	1 Love Vine overpowers, attacks stems leaves and draws nutrient from the host plant. 2 Mistletoe attacks stems and leaves and draws nutrient from the host plant to manufacture its own food supply.

Diseases	Examples	Effect on crops
Fungal	Damping off, leaf-spot, downy mildews, powdery mildews, soft rot, dry rot.	Damage to plant tissues causing loss of chlorophyll, rotting and decomposition.
Viral	Mosaic diseases, e.g. Cowpea mosaic, Tobacco mosaic.	Yellow mottling and crinkling of leaves, stunted growth, reduced yields.
Bacterial	1 Bacterial wilt in tomato and melongene. 2 Black rot in cabbage.	Plant wilts and dies. Rotting and decomposition.
Nematode	Root knot in tomato, lettuce and celery.	Blocks vascular system, stunted growth, reduced yields.

Methods of pest and disease control

There are several methods of controlling pests and diseases in crops. These may be classified as follows: chemical; biological; mechanical; and cultural.

Chemical Control

Now read Appendix 1: Safe use of agricultural chemicals on page 183.

Weedicides

A wide range of chemicals, known as weedicides, are used in the control of weeds. They are grouped according to their mode of action.

Insecticide application using a knap-sac sprayer. Note the use of safety equipment by the operator

Contact weedicides, e.g. *Paraquat, Roundup*

These weedicides act on contact. They destroy the chlorophyll present in leaves and young shoots but do not kill the hard stems or roots.

Systemic, e.g. *Karmex*

The chemical is absorbed into the plant system by means of the roots or other parts of the plant. As a result death occurs.

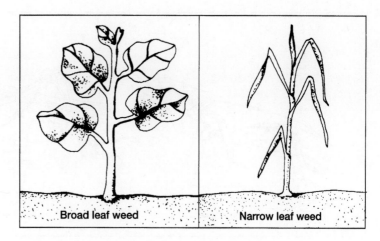

Broad leaf weed | Narrow leaf weed

Selective and non-selective weedicides

Selective weedicides kill some plants, but do not have any effect on other plants. For example *2,4-D* kills broad leaf weeds but does not kill narrow leaf weeds, such as grasses.

A non-selective weedicide destroys all types of weeds. *Gramoxone* is a good example of a non-selective weedicide.

Pre-emergent weedicides, e.g. *Atrazine, Dacthal*

Pre-emergent weedicides are sprayed on the soil after planting but before seed germination begins. The chemical delays the germination and growth of weeds but has no effect on the planted seed.

Now try to find out what is a post-emergent weedicide.

Rodenticides

Rats and mice are the chief animal pests of stored grains or grain crops in the field. Rodenticides, such as *Warfarin* and *Brumoline*, are commonly used in the preparation of poisoned baits for these rodents.

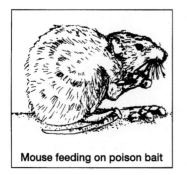

Mouse feeding on poison bait

Insecticides

Insecticides are used in the control of insect pests. These chemicals are grouped according to their mode of action.

Stomach poisons, e.g. lead arsenate

Lead arsenate is used in the preparation of baits mainly for **biting** or chewing insects, such as mole-crickets and grasshoppers. The insects feed on the poisoned bait and die.

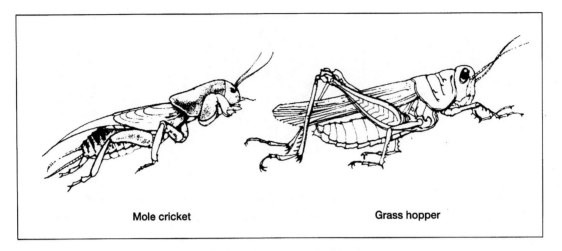

Mole cricket   Grass hopper

Contact insecticides, e.g. *Malathion, Diazinon*
Contact insecticides affect the nervous system of the insect
once it gets in contact with the chemical. These chemicals
are very effective against boring or **sucking** insects, such as
aphids, whiteflies, flea beetles and lacewing bugs.

Fumigants, e.g. carbon disulphide
Fumigants take effect in the gaseous state. They act on the
respiratory system of the insect thus affecting the assimila-
tion of oxygen, that is, the use of oxygen by the organism.

Control of plant diseases
The main disease causing organisms in plants are fungi,
bacteria, nematodes and viruses. The first three are controlled by fungicides, bactericides and nematicides respectively. There are several brands of these chemicals
obtainable in our garden shops.

Virus diseases are generally controlled by cultural methods which will be dealt with later in the lesson.

Disadvantages of using agricultural chemicals
There are several disadvantages and harmful effects result-
ing from the injudicious use of agricultural chemicals.
These may occur in the following ways.

1 The spray operator is likely to suffer skin injury or even
   poisoning if not properly garbed or equipped with proper
   spraying gears. Residual quantities of chemicals may
   accumulate in the body which become harmful when
   they reach a certain level.

2 By not using the correct chemical or the correct dosage, the crop sprayed is likely to suffer injury or may even be destroyed completely.

3 The presence of residual chemical substances in harvested crops could be harmful to the consumer.

4 When spraying against harmful insect pests, it is likely that useful insects to the farmer, such as bees, could also be destroyed.

5 Spray particles as well as the improper disposal of excess or waste chemicals tend to pollute water courses and atmospheric conditions. As a result the people and animals around could be affected.

6 Very often, the high cost.of chemicals makes them uneconomical for use in crop production programmes.

Biological control

Some animal pests and harmful insects have natural enemies. For example, cats destroy rats, mice and birds, frogs and lizards destroy insects, whilst ladybird beetles feed on certain types of ants, mealybugs, aphids and scale insects. The mud wasp captures and paralyses caterpillars which it places in its nest as feed for its grubs when they are hatched. These natural enemies should be encouraged and not destroyed.

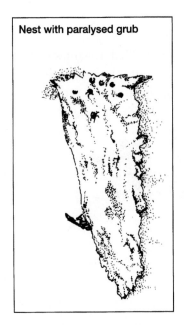

Nest with paralysed grub

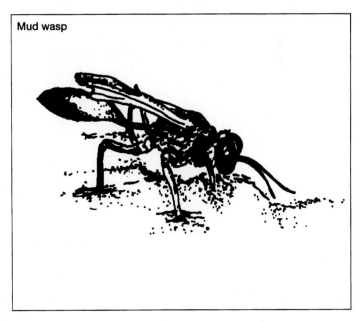

Mud wasp

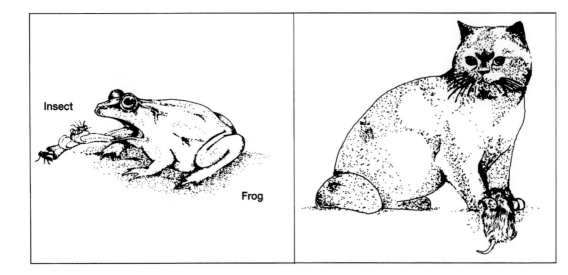

Insect

Frog

Mechanical or physical control

There are several mechanical or physical methods we can employ.

Hand picking

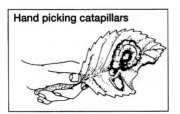

Hand picking catapillars

Caterpillars may be removed by hand and destroyed.

Use of sticky papers

Insects fly and rest on sticky papers. The insects become stuck there and die.

Use of traps

Sticky paper

The insect or animal is trapped and killed. Examples include: traps for insects, such as fruit flies; glue traps for mice; and heavy wooden spring type traps for rats.

Spring trap

Cultural methods

Cultural practices are important in the control of pests and diseases. Some of these practices are described below

Crop rotation

You will remember that crop rotation is the practice of growing different crops in succession on the same plot of land. Certain families of crops are generally attacked by a particular pest of disease. By rotating crops the pest population or disease is not allowed to build up and so is kept under control.

Sanitation

Garden plots and the surrounding areas should be kept free from weeds as weeds tend to harbour harmful insects. In cultivated crops, old leaves should be removed and disease infested branches pruned. Infected plant material should be buried or preferably burnt.

Selection of resistant varieties

Some crop varieties are more hardy and resistant to diseases and pest attacks than other varieties. Where possible, resistant varieties should be selected for cultivation.

Rogueing

In the process of rogueing, all plants infested with diseases, especially virus diseases such as cowpea and tobacco mosaic, are uprooted and destroyed by burying or burning.

Change of locality

Pests and diseases of a particular crop tend to build up over a period of time. When this happens, it becomes desirable to cultivate the crop in another locality where the pests or diseases may be absent.

Integrated pest management

In this lesson we learnt that there are several ways of controlling pests and diseases in crops. However, many farmers tend to rely completely on chemical control. Integrated pest management emphasises the use of all the methods of pest and disease control in crop protection. The physical, biological and cultural methods should be given priority. Chemicals should be used as a last resort, that is, when the pest population becomes high or the disease becomes widespread and too damaging.

Think of *two* reasons why the integrated pest management approach in plant protection is preferable to the use of chemicals alone.

Summary

There are several harmful organisms of the environment which attack our crops as pests or diseases. The main types of pests are weeds, insects, animals and plant parasites. Diseases are caused mainly by fungi, viruses, bacteria and nematodes. Pests and diseases are largely responsible for reducing the yield and quality of crops which ultimately affect the level of the farmer's income.

There are several methods of controlling pests and diseases in crops. These may be classified as chemical, biological, mechanical and cultural.

Chemical control of pests and diseases include the use of weedicides, insecticides, rodenticides, fungicides, bactericides and nematicides. These chemicals may be used as poisoned baits for controlling rodents and certain insect pests or as sprays in the control of weeds, insects and plant diseases.

It must be remembered that there are several disadvantages and harmful effects arising out of the injudicious use of chemicals. Some of these effects are poisoning, residual accumulations in plant and animals bodies, destruction of useful organisms and the pollution of water courses and atmospheric conditions. Chemicals are often very costly and may not be economical for use.

However, if it becomes necessary to use chemicals, several safety measures must be observed. These measures relate to the selection of chemicals, the preparation and use of spray mixtures, the use of safety clothing and equipment, spraying procedures, the safe storage of chemicals and the proper disposal of excess or waste spray mixtures.

In biological control the natural enemies of insect and animal pests are encouraged whereas in mechanical control such methods as hand picking and the use of traps and sticky papers are employed.

Cultural practices include measures such as crop rotation, sanitation, rogueing, selection of resistant varieties and the change of locality.

Farmers are advised to use the integrated pest management approach in the control of pests and diseases. This approach emphasises that biological, mechanical and cultural control measures should be given priority over chemical control. Chemicals should be used as a last resort, and that is, when the pest population builds up to excessive numbers or the disease becomes rampant.

Remember these

Biting insects	Insects whose mouth parts consist of jaws for biting and cutting.
Compatible	Able to exist together.
Cultivar	A crop variety, commercially selected, with known characteristics.
Mosaic diseases	Virus diseases usually recognised by stunted growth and yellow mottling of the leaves.
Parasite	An organism which lives on and obtains its nutrition from its host.
Pollution	Destruction of the pure state.
Post-emergent weedicide	A weedicide which is applied after weed growth takes place.
Rogueing	The uprooting and removal of disease infected plants from a cultivated plot.
Sucking insect	Insects whose mouth parts consist of a proboscis, that is, a tube like structure for sucking.
Vascular system	The transport system in a plant consisting of the xylem vessels and phloem elements.

Practical activities

1 Take a walk around your school farm and collect *three* examples of each (a) broad leaf weeds and (b) narrow leaf weeds. State their common and scientific names
2 Examine the crops in your garden plots and collect *six* different types of insects found in that locality. Study them carefully and then complete the table below:

Name of Insect	State whether useful or harmful	State how they are useful or harmful
1		
2		
3		
4		
5		
6		

3 Select two garden plots that are overgrown with different types of weeds. Label them A and B. Your farm attendant will spray plot A with *Gramoxone* and plot B with *2,4-D*. Observe the plots on the third day after spraying.
   a State the effect of the weedicides on the weeds in plots A and B.
   b Which of the two weedicides is best suited for weed control on a pasture?

Do these test exercises

1 **Select the best answer from the choices given.**

a Which of these is a sucking insect?
A locust.
B aphid.
C mole cricket.
D bachac.

b A farmer is advised to control the insect pests in his garden by their natural enemies. This method of control is described as
A biological.
B cultural.
C mechanical.
D chemical.

c A few cowpea plants in a garden plot showed stunted growth with yellow mottling and crinkling of the leaves. The disease causing organism is
A a fungus.
B a bacterium.
C a virus.
D a nematode.

d A weedicide was applied as control after weed growth had already taken place. Such a weedicide is described as
A selective.
B non-selective.
C pre-emergent.
D post-emergent.

2 **State the harmful effects of each of the following on garden crops:**
a Weed infestation.
b Insect attacks.
c Plant parasites.
d Nematode infestation.

3 **Give two examples of each of the following in crops:**
a Fungal disease.
b Virus infection.
c Bacterial disease.

4 **Differentiate between the following types of weedicides:**
a Contact and systemic
b Selective and non-selective
c Pre-emergent and post-emergent.

5 **State the safety measures that should be taken with agricultural chemicals to avoid the following.**
a Injury and poisoning to the spray operator.
b Pollution of water courses and atmospheric conditions.
c The presence of chemical residues on harvested agricultural products.

6 **Explain to a farmer the concept of 'integrated pest management' and the advantages of using this approach in controlling garden pests and diseases.**

7 **Write a short essay on *one* of the following topics.**
a The dangers of using agricultural chemicals in controlling garden pests and diseases.
b The safe use of agricultural chemicals.
c Cultural practices employed in the control of garden pests and diseases.

5

Mechanisation on the farm I – some basic principles

Lesson objectives

Many agricultural operations are performed by farm machinery. In this chapter you are going to learn about some basic principles and concepts related to farm mechanisation. On completing this lesson you should be able to:

1 Explain basic mechanical concepts.

2 List the sources of energy available on a farm.

3 State the uses of energy derived from different sources.

4 Identify a few simple machines used in agriculture.

5 Explain the basic principles underlying the operation of simple machines.

6 Apply basic mechanical principles in simple calculations.

7 Construct models to demonstrate mechanical concepts.

The pictures on page 49 show you some types of work that are done on farms and plantations. Notice the force that is needed to push a wheel-barrow full of farm produce, or to push a log from the timber yard to the carrier of a saw-mill. The force required to do this work comes from energy.

Energy

Energy may be defined as the capacity to do work. Energy is never destroyed, but it could be changed from one state to another. For example, energy may be in the **potential** state, that is, the inactive form, such as energy stored in foods and fuels, or it may be in the active or **kinetic** form, such as movement or work done.

Sources of energy

Energy is obtained from a number of sources. However, you need to know that our main source of energy is the sun. Energy is obtained from the sun as heat or as light. The heat of the sun warms up the soil as well as the waters of rivers, lakes and seas thereby creating a suitable environment for the survival of plants and animals. The heat of the sun is also used in sundriers, such as trays and cocoa-houses, or in solar heating systems commonly found in some of the Caribbean islands.

Plants absorb light energy during the process of photosynthesis. The energy so absorbed is stored in the manufactured products of the plants or in their body tissues. Carbohydrates, fats, and proteins are the basic foods of people and animals, whilst the woody tissues of plants are used for cooking, heating and the firing of furnaces.

Plankton (masses of seaweeds) also use light energy in their photosynthetic processes. They are the chief source of foods for fishes and other sea organisms. During earthquakes or earth movements, these sea organisms are buried in deep channels in the mud. They are the origin of our natural gases and mineral oils which are an invaluable source of energy on the farm.

Energy from the sun (solar energy)

The diagram on the next page shows how energy is obtained from the sun. Study it carefully and answer the following:

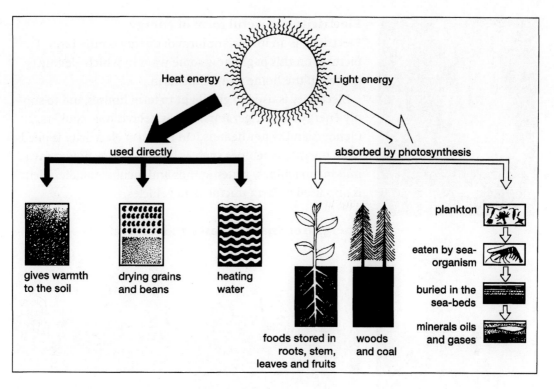

1 Name forms of energy that are obtained from the sun.
2 List ways in which the heat of the sun is used on a farm.
3 How do plants capture and store light energy?
4 How do animals obtain their energy supply from plants?

Energy from foods

People and animals obtain their energy supplies from the food they eat. Carbohydrates, fats, and proteins are all sources of energy. However, animals obtain the major part of their energy requirements from carbohydrates, that is, foods that are rich in sugars and starches.

Electricity – a useful form of energy

Electricity is an important form of energy on the farm. The pictures on this page show some ways in which electricity is used in the home and on the farm.

Electricity is used to give light to farm houses and to supply energy for refrigerators, radios, televisions, cookers, blenders and water heaters. On the farm electricity is needed to operate machines such as lawn mowers, power saws, milking machines, water pumps and incubators. Electricity is also used in farm tractors and vehicles.

Energy from natural gases and mineral oils

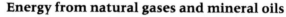

Oil is trapped in the earth with natural gases under high pressure. Huge pipes or casings are driven through the earth to the oil beds and the pressure of the gas forces the oil up the pipes. The oil is then pumped to the refinery where it is distilled into fuels, such as gasoline, kerosine, and diesel oil. Other products obtained in the process are lubricating oils, greases, paraffin wax, and hydrocarbons.

Other sources of energy

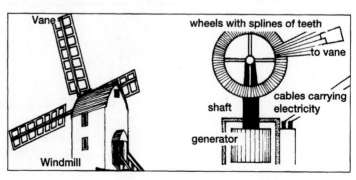

Wind and water are two other sources of energy. The remains of old windmills can still be seen at some of our sugar-cane factories, where wind energy assisted in the grinding process or in turning large wheels with **turbines** which generated electricity.

The energy from rapids and waterfalls is still used in some countries to generate electricity. In the Caribbean and surrounding countries water-power is not yet developed because our rivers do not maintain a steady flow of water throughout the year.

Force, work and power

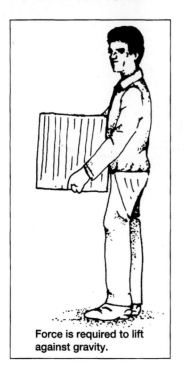

Force is required to lift against gravity.

Force

We have looked at energy and the various sources from which energy is obtained. When energy is used to influence the behaviour of an object in the form of movement, or when it is used in performing work, then force is exerted. Force can start or stop an object from moving. It can change its speed, its direction of movement as well as its shape. There are two major forces which act on an object. These are the forces of gravity and air pressure. Let us look more closely at gravity and its effect on objects around.

Gravity

When a ripe mango is detached from a tree it falls to the ground. It is pulled by a force called gravity. This force acts on the object as a whole and it seems to be focused to a particular point termed the centre of gravity. This centre of gravity is important in maintaining the stability of an object. For example, in a stationary vehicle standing on flat

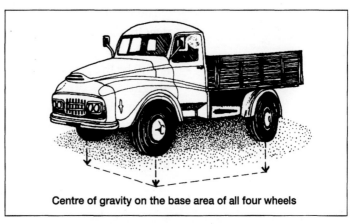

Centre of gravity on the base area of all four wheels

ground the centre of gravity is vertically over the support-
ing base area provided by the four wheels and so the
vehicle is stabilised. Now can you tell what is likely to happen when a tractor is pulling a loaded trailer on (a) gently
sloping ground and (b) very steep ground?

What effect does the centre of gravity have in these two
situations?

The force of gravity could be measured. In fact, the
weight of an object is the force with which it is attracted by
gravity. The greater the mass of the object the more strong-
ly will be the gravitational pull and the greater will be the
weight.

Weight is measured in newtons (N) in a scale which may
be of the lever arm type or a spring balance. You should
remember that an object with a mass of 100 g has a weight
of 1 N.

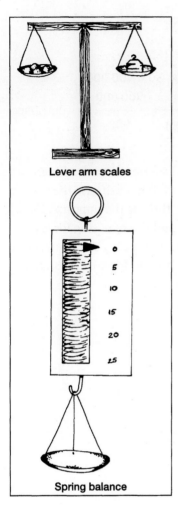

Lever arm scales

Spring balance

Work

Work is done when force is used to move or lift an object from one point to another. You will observe that the object is moved or lifted in the same direction of the force. Work is sometimes measured.

The unit of measurement for work is the joule (J). A joule is the force required to move a mass of one newton (100 g) over a distance of one metre.

Joule (J) = Mass in newtons × Distance in metres

Work   =   Force   × Distance
(in joules)   (in newtons) (in metres)

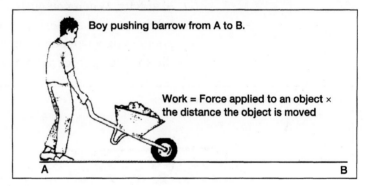

Boy pushing barrow from A to B.

Work = Force applied to an object × the distance the object is moved

A   B

Calculation

A box of bananas weighing 12 kg was moved over a distance of 20 m. Calculate the work done.

Work = Weight (in newtons) × Distance (in metres)
        = 120 × 20 = 2400 J.

Power

Power describes the amount of work that could be done in relation to time. For example, two people may do the same amount of work but over different periods of time. On the other hand a machine may do the same job in a shorter time.

Power is measured in watts. A watt is the rate of working at one joule per second.

$$\text{Power (in watts)} = \frac{\text{Work done (J)}}{\text{Time taken (sec)}} = \text{Joules/sec}$$

Calculation

A farmer moves 3000 kg of corn over a distance of 30 metres in 15 minutes. Calculate his power.

Weight = 3000 kg   = 30 000 N
Distance   = 30 m
Time   = 15 min
Work   = 30 000 × 30 = 900 000 J

$$\text{Power} = \frac{\text{Work (J)}}{\text{Time (sec)}} = \frac{900\,000}{900} = 1000 \text{ J/sec}$$

Friction

You will remember that work is done when you lift an object or when you push or pull it. In each case there is an opposing force. When you lift, there is the opposing force of gravity. When you push or pull the opposing force is friction. For example, if you push or pull a box of sweet-potatoes on a wooden floor, a friction force or resistance on the surface opposes the movement.

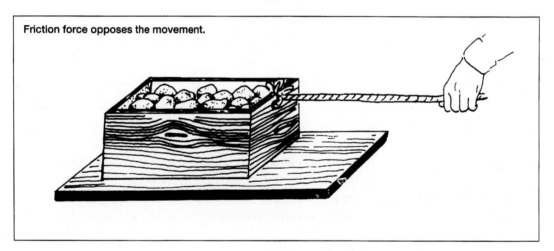
Friction force opposes the movement.

Friction could be defined as the resistance offered when one surface rubs or slides on another surface.

You will observe that the friction force or resistance is greater when the opposing surfaces of the objects are rough and dry or when the object that is pushed or pulled gets heavier.

The importance of friction

1 Can you grip and lift a bag without the force of friction?
2 How does the wheel of a tractor grip the ground when the tractor is at work?
3 What stops a vehicle in motion when the brakes are on?

The force of friction is always present during work or in movement of any type. It is through the force of friction

that a worker grips and lifts a bag or the wheels of a tractor grip the road. When brakes are applied the force of friction stops the vehicle from moving.

Name other situations in which friction is important.

Disadvantages of friction

Take two wooden or two metal objects and rub their surfaces together for a short while. You will observe that the surfaces become hot. Do you know why? It is because friction generates heat and later causes wear and tear of the objects. These disadvantages are very detrimental to machinery when they are in use. If not attended to, they could lead to further problems.

Reducing friction

The force of friction cannot be completely removed but it could be reduced. Try out the following exercises. It will help you to understand how the force of friction can be reduced.

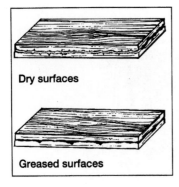

Dry surfaces

Greased surfaces

1 a Pull one object upon another ensuring that the surfaces which rub together are dry.
  b Do the same exercise as in (a) above but this time the surfaces which rub together must be greased.
2 a Pull a block of wood on a flat surface.
  b Pull a similar block as in 2(a) on rollers.
3 In which situations was the force of friction greater? Give explanations for your observations.
4 Now try to find out why ball bearings are used in the wheels of bicycles and motor vehicles.

It is often necessary to reduce the force of friction. This minimises the generation of heat and the wear and tear of moving parts, especially in machines and equipment that are made of metal. Friction is reduced by oiling and greasing and by ensuring that lubricating oil is present in the engine and transmission systems of motor vehicles, tractors and other farm machinery.

Simple machines

A machine is used for doing work and it can be described as any device which helps to make work easier. Let us look at some simple devices or machines used in agriculture for doing work.

Lever

The lever is a simple machine. It can help to lift or move an object. Study this diagram: it shows how a lever operates.

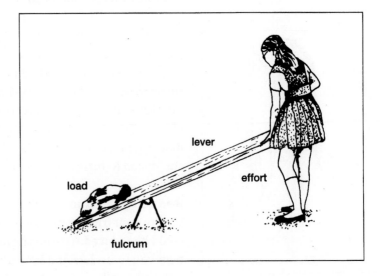

From the diagram you will notice that the lever consists of a bar. The object to be lifted or moved is the load, the force applied is the effort, and the point around which movement takes place is the **fulcrum**. When force is applied at the effort end the load is lifted and work is done.

Now try this exercise:

1 Set a permanent pivotal point on the ground. Get a wooden bar 2 m long and place a load of 10 kg on one end. Set the bar on the fulcrum (pivotal point) at a distance of 0.5 m away from the load and apply a force at the effort end to lift the load to a particular height.

2 Take a mental note of the effort that was needed.

3 Now do the same exercise but at distances of 1 m and 1.5 m from the fulcrum. You would observe that the effort exerted to lift the load increases as the distance from the fulcrum to the point of effort gets shorter.

Here are two examples of machines built on different

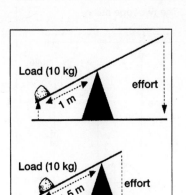

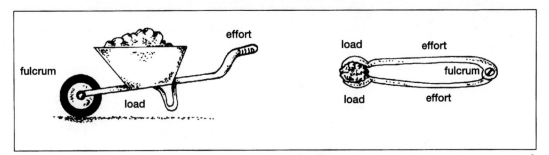

types of lever system. Observe the positions of the load, the fulcrum and the effort. Give reasons for your answers to the following questions:

1 What difference do you observe about the positions of (i) the fulcrum and (ii) the load in these two machines?

2 Which machine is better suited for (i) light work and (ii) heavy work?

Pulley

Pulleys are an arrangement of ropes and wheels. This machine is designed to lift a load at one end of the rope when the person pulls downward on the other end.

In a single pulley with one rope bearing the load the effort is the same as the load. Do you know why? It is because the distance the rope is pulled down is the same as the load is lifted.

In a two rope pulley system only half the effort is needed because the effort is applied through twice the distance to lift the load.

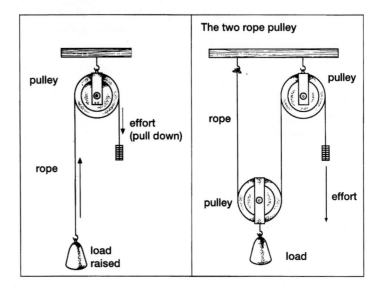

The two rope pulley

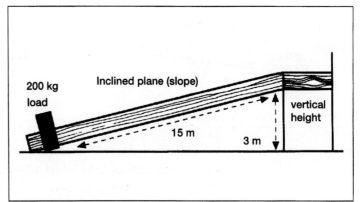

The incline plane (slope)

The diagram shows you the picture of an inclined plane. Observe the flat surface with one end higher than the other. It takes less effort to lift a 200 kg load up the plank to a height of 3 m than to lift the same load vertically to the same height.

Calculation

$$\text{Gradient} = \frac{\text{Vertical height}}{\text{Distance of slope}} = \frac{3}{15} = 3:15 = 1:5$$

There is a relationship between effort and load associated with the gradient of the slope: here the gradient is 1:5 and therefore the effort is 1/5 of the load.

Effort = 200 × 1/5 = 40 kg

Summary

Energy is defined as the capacity to do work. Energy may exist in the potential state as in foods and fuels or in the kinetic form as in movement and work done.

Our main source of energy is the sun. It provides heat energy for sun driers and solar systems and light energy which is then absorbed by plants during photosynthesis. The energy so absorbed is stored in the body tissues and the manufactured products of plants. These manufactured plant products are the food sources which supply us with the energy we need.

Other sources of energy on the farm are the woody tissues of plants, electricity, the products of natural gases and mineral oils and the energy derived from wind and water.

Force is exerted when energy is used to move an object or to perform work. However, the force exerted is opposed by other forces one of which is gravity. The force of gravity attracts an object to the earth and the point of focus, that is, the centre of gravity is important in stabilising objects. Gravity influences weight. As the mass of an object increases, the gravitational pull becomes greater and the weight of the object increases. Weight is measured in newtons, which is a weight of 100 g.

Work is the force required to move or lift an object from one point to another. It is the product of the force applied and the distance moved. The unit of measurement is the joule.

Power describes the amount of work that is done over a period of time. It is measured in watts. The rate of working at 1 watt equals one joule per second.

Friction is the resistance offered by opposing surface in movement. The force of friction increases with the roughness of the surfaces or with the increased weight of the object in movement. Friction is important in many ways. It enables us to grip things or to stop a vehicle in movement. It is the force of friction that helps the wheels of a tractor to grip the road. However, friction is dangerous to machinery.

It generates heat and causes wear and tear. This can be reduced by oiling, greasing and the use of lubricating oils in engines and transmission systems.

A machine is described as any device which helps to make work easier. Some of the simple machines used in agriculture are levers, pulleys and the inclined plane. In each of these devices the relationship is between the effort and the load with distance as an intervening factor.

Remember these

Energy	Capacity for work.
Friction	The resistance offered when one surface rubs or slides on another.
Fulcrum	The point on which a lever is placed to get support.
Gradient	The degree of slope on an inclined plane, a hillside or a roadway.
Gravity	The force of attraction which pulls an object towards the centre of the earth
Hydrocarbons	Compounds that are made up mainly of hydrogen and carbon.
Joule (J)	The force required to move a mass of one newton over a distance of one metre.
Kinetic energy	Energy in action such as in movement and in work.
Newton (N)	A weight of 100 g.
Potential energy	Energy in the inactive state as in foods and fuels.
Turbines	Rotary motors driven by water or by steam.
Watt (W)	The rate of working of one joule per second.

Practical activities

1 Locate a screeching door. Lubricate the hinges properly with oil or grease. Now swing the door again.
   a What difference do you observe?
   b Give reasons for the difference
2 a Get a jar with a screw top cover and screw on the cover very firmly. Take a dry cloth, grip the cover and unscrew it. Observe the force of friction.
   b Screw the cover on the jar as firmly as before. Now smear the cover, the jar and your hands with Vaseline and try unscrewing the cover without the use of the cloth and with the use of the cloth.
   In which of the two situations (dry or greased) is it easier to unscrew the cover? Explain why this is so.

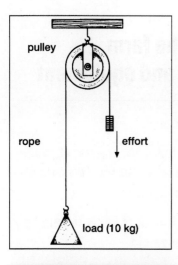

pulley

rope

effort

load (10 kg)

3 Collect either a pair of pliers or a pair of scissors. Make a drawing of the object and indicate the positions of (a) the load (b) the effort and (c) the fulcrum.
State the uses of this piece of equipment on a farm.

4 Set up a one rope pulley system like the one in the diagram. On completing the set up, pull the rope downward on the effort end to ensure that the system is working. State the effort required to pull a load of 10 kg; 25 kg; and 45 kg.

Do these test exercises

1 **Select the best answer from the choices given.**

a A newton is a weight of
A 200 g
B 150 g
C 100 g
D 50 g

b The joule is used as the unit of measurement for
A weight.
B work.
C power.
D energy.

2 **List three sources of energy supply on a farm. State two ways** in which energy is used from each of the sources mentioned.

3 **What is friction? Name two examples to illustrate the importance of friction and the disadvantages of friction.** Explain to a farmer the reasons for lubricating farm machinery.

4 **State whether the effort is likely to increase or decrease in the following situations. Give reasons for your answer.**

a When the distance between the fulcrum and the load is increased.

b When the gradient on an inclined plane is decreased from 1/3 to 1/6.

c When a two rope pulley is used to lift a load instead of a one rope pulley.

5 **Do these calculations:**

a A sack of sweet-potatoes weighing 16 kg was moved over a distance of 36 m. Calculate the work done.

b A farmer moved 72 kg of coffee beans over a distance of 240 metres in 15 minutes. Calculate the power.

c Calculate the effort that is required to push a barrel of fertiliser weighing 120 kg along an inclined plane 20 m in length and 4 m above the ground.

6

Mechanisation on the farm II – farm machinery and equipment

Lesson objectives

In this lesson you are going to learn about some of the machines and equipment used on our farms. On completing this lesson you should be able to:

1 List some advantages that a farmer is likely to gain by using farm machines and equipment.

2 Identify some machines and equipment used on farms.

3 Identify some of the external parts of a wheel tractor and state their functions.

4 Describe how power is produced in an internal combustion gas engine and transmitted for use in movement and work.

5 State the functions of specified farm machines and equipment.

6 Care for and maintain farm machines and equipment.

Tractor with seed planter

Farmers can carry out almost all agricultural operations from ploughing the fields to harvesting crops by means of machines. **Mechanisation** is important in agriculture as it reduces the amount of **manual labour** that farmers do in production practices. It is often more economical to do work on a large scale by machines than by manual labour.

Farmers can increase their income by improving the yields and the quality of crops they produce. In order to achieve this, farm machines are necessary because agricultural labour is often very expensive and in short supply.

The wheel tractor

The wheel tractor is one of the most important farm machines as these pictures show. It is used on large as well as on small farms.

Tractor and plough

Tractor and forage harvester

Tractor and sprayer

Tractor and trailer

Tractor and mower

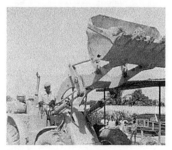

Tractor and front-lift bucket loader

Parts of a wheel tractor

This diagram shows you some of the external parts of a wheel tractor. Look at the parts very carefully and try to find them in a tractor. Each part of a tractor has its specific function to perform. We are going to study the functions of three major components of the wheel tractor – the engine, gearbox and differential.

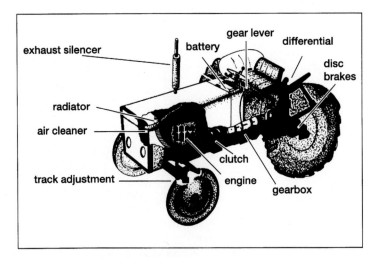

The engine

The engine is usually situated at the front end of the tractor. Its main function is to produce the power that the tractor needs. The diagram shows you a cross section of the

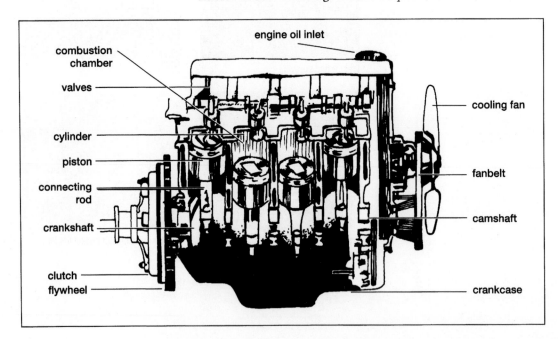

4 stroke internal combustion gas engine. Observe how the piston fits into the cylindrical opening of the engine block and is attached to the crankshaft by a connecting rod. At one end of the crankshaft is the flywheel. Above the piston is the combustion chamber where compressed gaseous fuel is ignited by an electric spark causing an explosion, thereby, releasing energy, carbon dioxide and water.

The energy produced is the source of power that is used to set the flywheel into rotary motion. The carbon dioxide and water are expelled through the **exhaust** as waste substances.

The gearbox

The gearbox transmits power from the engine to the differential. Within the gearbox there are shafts with gears and these are put into action by means of a gear shift and selectors. As a result, the desired power and speed are obtained. The gearbox is linked to the engine through the **clutch**. This unit is responsible for engaging the gear system to or disengaging it from the power source, that is, the flywheel in the engine. From the gearbox power is transmitted through the drive shaft to the differential.

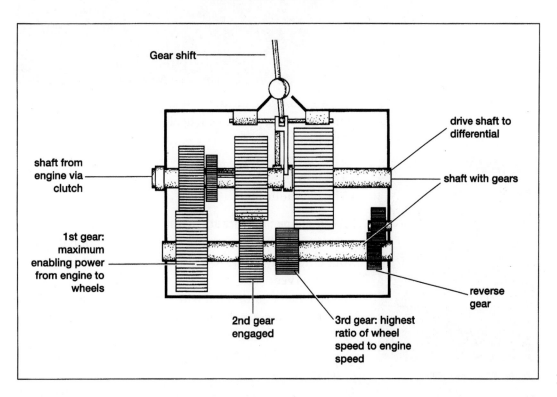

Gear shift

drive shaft to differential

shaft from engine via clutch

shaft with gears

1st gear: maximum enabling power from engine to wheels

2nd gear engaged

3rd gear: highest ratio of wheel speed to engine speed

reverse gear

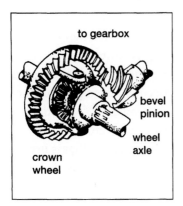

to gearbox

bevel
pinion

wheel
axle

crown
wheel

The differential

The differential consists of a crown wheel and pinions. It receives the power from the gearbox to rotate the wheels by means of the axles. As a result, movement takes place.

You will notice that a tractor can move from place to place and at the same time operate an implement.

Power from the engine is transmitted through the gearbox to the differential. The differential drives the rear wheels, allowing each of them to turn at different speeds. This enables the tractor to move and turn corners.

Power to work some of the implements comes from the power take-off shaft (picture below). This is an independent shaft, attached to the gearbox, engaged or disengaged by means of a special clutch.

Power take-off shaft

Now investigate further and try to find out the functions of the following parts in a wheel tractor:

1 The battery.
2 The brakes.
3 The power take-off shaft.
4 The hydraulic lift.

The care and maintenance of a tractor

A tractor must be given proper care and attention if it is to work efficiently and give good service. Here are ten points to be observed:

1 Keep the radiator filled with water when the tractor is at work. This water should be changed periodically.
2 The oil in the engine and the gearbox must be maintained at their correct level. Change the engine oil periodically.

Land preparation – ploughing

3 Tyre pressure must be checked regularly.

4 Batteries should be topped up with distilled water. Terminals must be firm and free from corrosion.

5 Horn and lights should be in proper working order.

6 Plugs and points or injectors should be cleaned regularly.

7 Brakes should be adjusted and kept in good working order at all times.

8 Fuels must be free from moisture and solid particles.

9 Wash and lubricate the tractor regularly. Replace worn out or defective parts.

10 Ensure that the tractor is licensed and insured each year.

Land preparation implements

The soil must be properly cultivated in order to grow good crops. Let us now look at some of the implements used in land preparation. These implements may be trailed or they may be mounted on to the tractor.

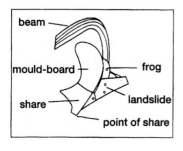

The plough

The chief function of the plough is to turn the soil over in furrows and leave it exposed to the air. There are two main types in use.

1 The mould-board plough

Look at the structure of the mould-board plough. It consists of the coulter, the plough share, the mould-board, and the rear wheel. These parts are attached to a beam.

The coulter cuts the soil vertically so as to give a clean furrow slice. The plough share cuts the soil horizontally, whilst the mould-board turns over the slice of soil. The rear wheels are adjustable and control the depth of the furrow.

The mould-board plough

2 The disc plough

Two or more discs are mounted or trailed behind the disc tractor. The discs roll along the ground and are adapted to work on heavy clayey soils or on rough stony grounds. Disc ploughs are also well suited for deep ploughing.

You will observe that the soil in a newly ploughed field is turned over in large clumps. In order to cultivate crops the farmer has to do further land preparation to refine the soil.

The disc plough

The rotavator (rotary plough)

Rotary ploughs are in common use in many Caribbean islands. It consists of a horizontal shaft on which there are cutting knives or tines. It is pulled by the tractor and powered by means of the power take-off shaft.

The rotary plough turns the soil to a depth of 10–15 cm and is generally used on newly ploughed lands to produce a soil with a fine tilth.

The rotavator

The harrow

There are several types of harrow. The picture shows you a disc harrow. This has a number of discs arranged in gangs of single or double rows. It may be trailed or mounted on the tractor.

The harrow is often used for cutting up vegetable matter on the ground before the land is ploughed. However, its chief function is to **pulverise** the field after it is ploughed and to prepare the ground for planting.

Disc harrow

The hand-guided tractor

Here is a picture of the hand-guided tractor. It is motor driven and different attachments are fitted for ploughing, rotavating or harrowing the field. It may also be used for other operations, such as planting and spraying, or for mowing lawns. This tractor is best suited for work on small vegetable farms. It reduces labour cost and increases crop production. It must be noted, too, that the hand-guided tractor is not as costly as the wheel tractor.

The hand-guided, motor driven tractor

Sowing and harvesting machines

Sowing machines

There are several types of machine for sowing and harvesting crops.

On small farms hand sowing may be replaced by simple mechanical machines. On large plantations more elaborate machines are needed.

The panga, a simple mechanical aid for planting

A simple seed planter

A four-furrow seed planter, tractor mounted

The machine in the left-hand picture is used for planting corn. It is **calibrated**, that is, it is adjusted to open furrows and to sow the correct number of seeds at both a uniform depth and the desired spacing. It also covers the seeds after they are sown. These machines can be used for planting other seeds, such as peas and beans.

Harvesting machines

Many of our crops are harvested by machine. The corn harvester gathers and snaps ears of corn, and then husks and shells them. The corn harvester works best on flat or on gently undulating land. The ground must be well prepared and the corn planted in rows, spaced to suit the machine.

The corn harvester

It is important to choose a good variety of corn. Such varieties have stiff stalks that do not fall over. The ears must be large and tough and the grains firm and rigid.

Look at the sugar-cane farmers at harvest time. They cut the canes, top them off, and load them on trucks for transport. The sugar-cane harvester performs the same operations by means of cutting knives and a conveyor belt. The canes are harvested, chopped into small lengths, and loaded on to trucks which move alongside the harvester as it works. (See chapter 4.) Now tell why:

1 sugar-cane harvesters are desirable on very large plantations;

2 farmers with small plantations do not own harvesting machines.

In your own country you may see machines suitably designed for harvesting other crops such as sweet-potatoes, paddy, cotton, carrots, peas and beans and fodder grasses.

Sugar-cane harvester

The fertiliser spreader

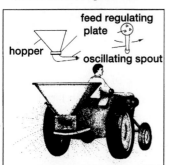

There are several designs of machine for spreading manure, broadcasting fertilisers and applying liquid fertiliser sprays. This picture shows you a fertiliser spreader. It consists of a hopper, a feed-regulating plate, and an oscillating spout. The hopper is filled with fertiliser, which is fed through the regulating plate into the oscillating spout. This broadcasts the fertiliser granules evenly over the field.

What are the advantages of a fertiliser spreader over the broadcasting of fertiliser by hand?

Spraying and dusting equipment

Our crops are affected by disease, insect attack and weed infestation. These are controlled by dusting or by spraying with chemicals dissolved in water.

Look at the types of duster and sprayer. They vary in size and in operation, from the simple mechanical type to the more elaborate, engine-driven type.

Many farmers use mechanical sprayers which are hand operated. Look at the parts of the pressure-pump sprayer in the picture below. It consists of a tank, a pump and a spray gun which is attached to the tank by means of a rubber hose. There are filters to strain the liquid and several rubber gaskets to prevent the escape of air and the leakage of liquids. The plunger in the pump is fitted with a leather packing.

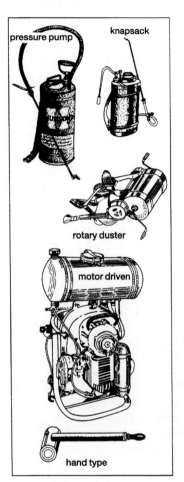

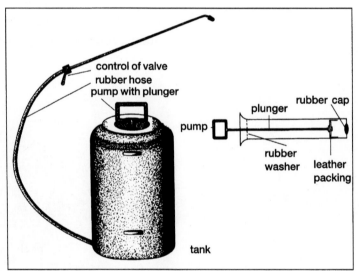

In preparation for spraying, the spray mixture is placed in the tank and pressured by the pump. Under high pressure the liquid enters the delivery hose, that is, the rubber hose, to the spray gun by means of the control valve. The size and spread of the spray droplets are controlled by adjusting the spray nozzle.

The milking machine

The milking machine is a useful piece of equipment on dairy farms when there are 12 or more cattle in **lactation**, that is, in milk production. The machine, designed to extract the milk from the cow, by a process similar to the sucking action of the calf.

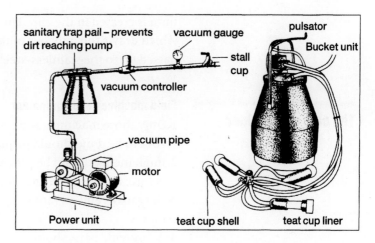

The bucket-type milking machine is commonly used on small dairy farms. Its chief components are a power unit, a vacuum pump, the teat-cup assembly, the pulsator and a stainless-steel bucket.

The power unit works the vacuum pump which removes air from the system, whilst the **pulsator** provides a rhythmic breathing action by an alternate removal and intake of air supply.

Each teat cut consists of a metal outer case fitted with an inner rubber liner. Between the rubber liner and the outer metal case there is a chamber which is connected to the pulsator.

The four teat cups are attached to the cow's teats. When air is withdrawn from the teat-cup chamber, a partial vac-

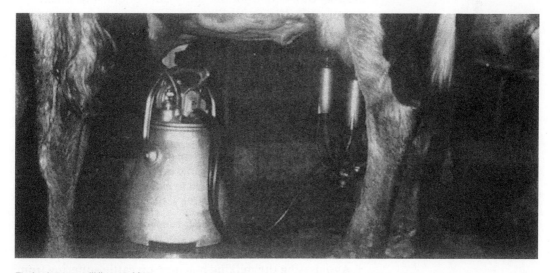

The bucket-type milkling machine

uum is created in the cup. This produces a sucking action which draws the milk out of the teat. The milk is then passed on to the stainless-steel bucket on the floor.

The care of machines

Field machines and equipment

1 Only those machines and implements best suited for the work to be done should be purchased.
2 Implements should be properly mounted and adjusted before, as well as during, work.
3 Gearboxes and oil tanks should be filled to their proper marks.
4 All moving parts should be well greased and **lubricated**. **Check** machines and implements regularly. Tighten bolts, nuts and screws that are loose. Replace parts that are worn, broken, or missing.
5 Implements should be washed free form dirt. When not in use, they should be oiled, greased and stored in a covered shed.

Dusters and sprayers

1 If possible, use separate sprayers for insecticides and weedicides. The can should be washed several times with a detergent when changing from weedicides to insecticides.
2 Always wash the can and flush it with clean water after use.
3 Mixtures should not be left to stand overnight in the spray can. Unmount the spray can periodically. Clean, grease, and replace missing or worn-out parts, such as jets, rubber gaskets and leather packings.

Milking machine care

1 Ensure stric sanitation. The machine should be thoroughly washed and sterilised after each milking.
2 Check pulsator and teat cups regularly. Keep them in good order.
3 The pulsator should not be operated at too fast or too slow a rate.
4 Hoses should be cleaned and kept free from cracks and leaks.
5 The vacuum line should be inspected and cleaned two or three times a year.
6 Avoid using the milking machine on cattle suffering from diseases of the udder, such as mastitis.

Summary

Mechanisation is important in agriculture. It reduces the need for manual labour and is often very economical. As a result of mechanisation farm yields are increased and ultimately the farmer's income is also increased.

The wheel tractor is one of the most important machines on large as well as on small farms. It performs a wide range of agricultural activities from land preparation to harvesting.

Farmers who own tractors should have a knowledge of the structure and operation of their tractors, the implements used and the care and management practices essential for maintaining the tractor and its attachments.

Land preparation implements include the plough, the rotavator and the harrow. The mould-board and disc ploughs turn over the soil in large clumps whilst the refining is done by the rotavator and the harrow.

On small vegetable farms, the hand-guided tractor is an important piece of equipment.

Sowing and harvesting machines range from very simple machines used on small farms to more complex ones used on large farms. These machines must be properly calibrated for the work they have to perform. It is also important, that land preparation and production practices be designed to facilitate the operations of these machines.

Fertiliser spreaders are designed for spreading manure, broadcasting fertilisers or applying liquid fertiliser sprays. The machine should be properly regulated so that the fertiliser is spread evenly over the field.

Spraying and dusting equipment are needed for controlling weeds, insect pests and diseases. Some of these are simple hand-operated machines while the more sophisticated ones are motor driven. Where practicable separate spray cans should be used for weedicides and insecticides.

Milking machines are essential on dairy farms with 12 or more animals in lactation. These machines extract the milk from the cow in a process similar to the sucking action of the calf. A milking machine is made up of several components which should be well regulated and working satisfactorily. The farmer should ensure that the machine is thoroughly washed and sterilised after each milking.

Remember these

Calibrated   Adjusted to obtain a combination of activities in the correct order and at the correct time.

Clutch   The mechanism which engages a system to or disengage it from another.

Exhaust   An outlet in the engine system through which burnt gases are expelled.

Harrow   A land preparation equipment with tines or knives for reducing the soil to a fine tilth.

Lactation   Milk production.

Lubricate   To apply oil or grease so as to reduce friction.

Manual labour   Work done by hand.

Mechanisation   The use of machines to replace manual labour.

Pulsator   A mechanism which provides the breathing action for the alternate removal and intake of air supply.

Pulverise   To reduce to very fine particles.

Practical activities

1 Examine the tools in your agriculture unit or tool room.
   a Identify three pieces of equipment designed for manual use.
   b State the functions of the equipment identified in (a) above.
   c Name the machines or equipment that replace the tools identified in (a) in a mechanisation programme.

2 Visit a nearby farm or agriculture station and observe a wheel tractor. Identify the parts of the tractor shown in the labelled diagram on page 66.

3 Your teacher will place the differential of a wheel tractor or motor vehicle in your classroom for observation.
   a Identify the crown wheel and pinions.
   b State whether the axles are attached to the crown wheel or pinions.
   c Explain how power from the drive shaft is transferred to the wheels.

4 Visit any *one* of the following farms or plantations and make a list of the machines and implements that are used on the farm:
   a A dairy farm.
   b A pig farm.
   c A vegetable farm.
   d A sugar-cane plantation.

Do these test exercises

1 Select the best answer from the choices given.

a In a wheel tractor, the main source of power to do work comes from
A the battery.
B the engine.
C the gearbox.
D the differential.

b The implement used for pulverising the soil is the
A disc plough.
B mould-board plough.
C rotavator.
D harrow.

c The implement best adapted to work on heavy clayey soils is the
A harrow.
B rotavator.
C disc plough.
D mould-board plough.

d A farmer operating a trouble-free pressure pump sprayer decided to widen the spread of the spray droplets. This was achieved by
A increasing the amount of spray mixture in the tank.
B adjusting the nozzle at the end of the spray gun.
C increasing the opening at the control valve.
D lowering the spray gun while spraying.

e The pulsator is a component of
A the fertiliser spreader.
B the corn harvester.
C the pressure pump sprayer.
D the milking machine.

2 A farmer cultivates vegetables on 1 hectare of good loamy soil. What do you consider to be the most suitable machine that should be purchased to cultivate this land?
Give reason for your answer.

3 Explain the following in your own words:
a A corn sower must be calibrated.
b Sugar-cane should not be planted at random.
c A mechanically operated sprayer.
d Animals in lactation

4 What functions do the following perform
a The battery in a vehicle.
b The power take-off shaft in a tractor.
c The ploughshare in a mould-board plough.
d The pulsator in a milking machine.

5 Say why
a Farm implements that are not in use should be greased.
b Moving parts in a machine should be lubricated.
c Rubber hoses in a milking machine must be free from cracks and leaks.
d Cattle suffering from mastitis should not be milked with the milking machine.

6 Say how
a Ploughing improves soil fertility
b Pressure is built up in a spray can.
c A tractor supplies power to a rotavator.
d Farm machines help to increase farm incomes.

7 Write a shot paragraph on each of the following:
a Agricultural mechanisation is helpful to a farmer.
b The reasons why many farmers do not own or machines on their farms.

7

Some systems of farming

Lesson objectives

The efficient use of natural and human resources in agricultural production depends to a great extent upon the system of farming that is in practice. On completing this lesson you should be able to:

1 Name some systems of farming practised in the Caribbean.

2 Give simple descriptions of the farming systems named in (1) above.

3 Differentiate between farming systems.

4 State the advantages that a farmer is likely to gain by practising mixed farming.

5 Identify the problems associated with shifting cultivation.

6 Prepare a model to demonstrate a farming system.

Many people who live in rural areas are farmers. Some of them are farm owners, whilst others may be employed on farms.

Farmers grow crops and rear animals. They rely on natural and human resources such as soil, weather conditions, planting materials, labour, capital and management practices. The efficient use of these resources depends upon the farming system employed. Let us look at some of the farming systems which exist in the Caribbean and other tropical countries.

Intensive and extensive systems

Mr Garcia's pig farm (see page 81) is operated **intensively**. Mr Garcia aims to get high returns or profits by rearing large numbers of animals within a limited amount of space and over short periods of time.

Intensive pig farming

An intensively run animal farm involves high capital input. Farm buildings and houses must be well designed and constructed. Good breeds of animals must be selected and they should be adequately fed and watered. Sanitation and good health measures are absolutely essential.

Field and vegetable crops may also be cultivated intensively. Mr Jones operates his vegetable garden on an intensive scale. He spends large sums of money on tools and equipment and makes efficient use of fertilisers and plant protection chemicals, such as insecticides, fungicides and nematicides. He introduces improved crop varieties producing good quality crops that are high yielding and disease resistant.

Extensive cattle rearing

Mrs Ramdeen rears cattle on an **extensive** scale. Her animals do not need elaborate houses. They are allowed to roam in the fields and pastures where they feed and take care of themselves. The farmer herds or collects her animals whenever necessary. In a similar way crops may be established or allowed to grow at random. Mr Burton harvests cocoa crops year after year without much concern about the use of fertilisers or the control of pests and diseases. The yield and the quality of his cocoa crops are generally poor. Tell why his crops give poor yields.

Extensive cocoa crop production

In extensive farming large areas of land several hectares in size are employed. The capital output is generally very low and highly skilled labour is not essential.

Tell why this system of farming is not desirable in the Caribbean.

The plantation system

The pictures (top page 83) show you some tropical crops that are grown in plantations. There are other plantation crops which you may know about.

A **plantation** consists of many hectares of land cultivated with only one main crop. On a plantation, there are several employees, many of whom are technically trained. Large sums of money are invested in tools and machines. This equipment is used in field preparation, planting out, fertilising, spraying, harvesting and processing. The raw materials, as well as the manufactured products of the

Banana – a plantation crop

Cocoa – a plantation crop

Coffee – a plantation crop

plantation, may be sold in the local markets or exported to foreign countries.

Some large plantations have their own research and experiment stations. They employ security forces and offer medical and social services to their employees.

Now make a list of the crops which grow in plantations in your country.

Mixed farming

Mr Toolsie operates a mixed farm. Do you know what a mixed farm is? **Mixed farming** has several advantages. You can find these out by studying the diagram on the next page.

A mixed farm

You will observe that mixed farming involves the growing of crops and the rearing of animals on the same farm.

Mixed farming helps Mr Toolsie to use his lands more efficiently. The crops he grows and the animals he rears provide him with food, clothing, shelter and work.

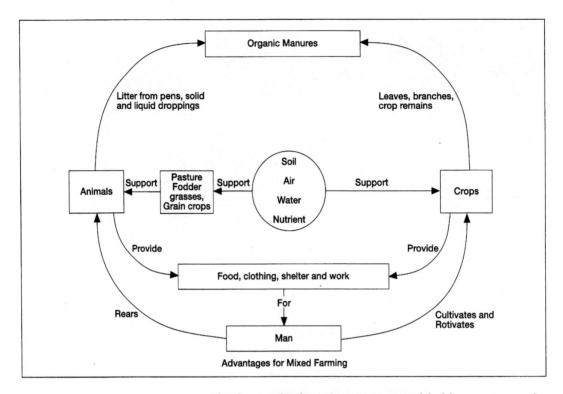

Advantages for Mixed Farming

The farmer feeds grains, pasture and fodder grasses, and the remains of crops to the farm animals, whilst the excreta and litter from the animal pens are incorporated with plant residues to form **organic manures**. These manures are added to the soil to increase its fertility and to improve the growth of plants.

In operating a mixed farm the farmer often cultivates a variety of crops. This enables rotation of crops to make maximum use of soil nutrients, control pests and diseases and maintain soil fertility. The farm also provides regular employment for employees and at the same time the farmer has a good and regular income.

Subsistence farming

Mr Krishen is employed in a factory. Some of his friends work in government service and in commercial banks. However, they also own small parcels of land on which they practise **subsistence farming**. They grow a few crops and rear a few animals to assist with the family food requirements and to supplement their earnings. Subsistence farming is an effort of the whole family and is usually pursued during leisure hours, weekends and public holidays.

Working in a factory

Subsistence farming

Shifting cultivation

Shifting cultivation is a type of farming developed by primitive communities and is still practised in many developing countries in Asia, tropical Africa, Central and South America and parts of the Caribbean.

Observe the hillsides and forested regions of your country. You may notice portions of land cultivated with short-term crops. You may also see areas of secondary forest growth: these are lands that were once cultivated but are now abandoned. On such lands there is a regrowth of forest trees that are often evidence of shifting cultivation.

Short-term crops planted on cleared forest land

Farmer Singh clears the land by cutting and burning. He plants a cereal crop, such as corn, and follows this with pigeon pea, banana and root crops like yam, tannia, eddoe, cassava and sweet potato.

The farmer relies on the natural fertility of the soil and does not use manures or fertilisers. The land is not ploughed but is worked with simple tools such as hoes, cutlasses and digging forks.

Farmer Singh continues this cultivation for a period of 8 to 10 years and then abandons the field to lie fallow and regenerate its fertility under natural vegetation for a period of 20 to 25 years. He then clears a new plot of forested land for cultivation. The following diagram shows you how the cycle of shifting cultivation works.

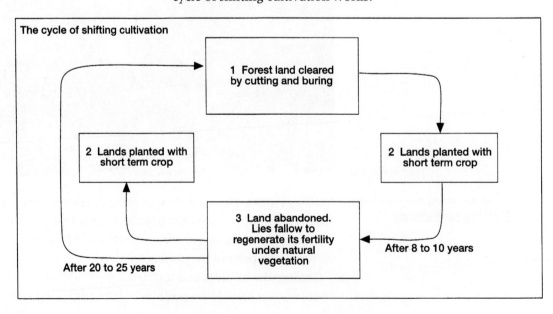

The cycle of shifting cultivation

1 Forest land cleared by cutting and buring

2 Lands planted with short term crop

2 Lands planted with short term crop

3 Land abandoned. Lies fallow to regenerate its fertility under natural vegetation

After 8 to 10 years

After 20 to 25 years

The problems of shifting cultivation

There are many problems associated with the practice of shifting cultivation. This system of farming leads to the destruction of natural resources including useful forest trees and animal life. In the process of burning the land, organic matter in the form of surface litter is destroyed and the soil is exposed to erosion. As a result, valuable soil nutrients are lost by leaching and the fertility of the soil is reduced. Ultimately crop yields and crop quality are also reduced.

Shifting cultivation is an undesirable practice in any country, but more so in the Caribbean where many of our islands are small and our natural resources are limited.

Specialised farming units

Many farmers prefer to operate specialised farm units. In these units they concentrate on a single agricultural enterprise. Mr Suresh cultivates market garden crops whilst Mr Baker is a specialist in the production of broiler birds.

Vegetables in a market garden

A farmer operating a specialised farm unit must have specific knowledge and training. Specific tools and equipment are needed for the particular enterprise. In a special farm enterprise, it is often easy to organise, manage and control labour. However, it must be operated intensively to bring favourable returns. Farm products are often produced abundantly and economically. As a result, a farmer is better able to supply the marketing agencies.

A poultry enterprise of broiler production

Summary

The efficient use of natural and human resources in agricultural production depends largely upon the farming system in practice. In an intensive system, the aim is to obtain high returns within a short period of time with limited land resources. Such a system requires high capital inputs, well designed farm buildings and houses, and high levels of management skills.

In an extensive system, large areas of lands are involved but with little capital and low management inputs. In this system, the yield and quality of agricultural products are usually poor.

Some crops, such as bananas, sugar-cane, cocoa and coffee, are grown in large plantations. In the plantation system a large land area is planted with only one main crop. There is high capital investment in machines and equipment, skilled labour, training, research, security and social services. The raw and manufactured products of plantation crops are used in the local markets or exported to foreign countries.

Many farmers operate mixed farms on which crops are grown and animals are reared. From these the farmers obtain their livelihood. The crops and animals support each other: the grains and remains of crops are fed to the animals; the animals, in return, supply manure which is used as fertiliser to the crops. Mixed farming also enables the farmer to practise crop rotation, keep workers in regular employment and earn a regular income.

The subsistence farmer is employed in a job other than farming, but, engages in farming during leisure hours, weekends and holidays. The aim is to meet some of the family food requirements and to supplement earnings.

Shifting cultivation is the practice of slashing and burning forest lands for the cultivation of short-term crops. There is very little or no capital input. When the crop yield and quality fall the farmer abandons the land and moves on to a new area of forested land and continues the cycle. This system of farming is undesirable as it leads to the destruction of natural resources and exposes the land to erosion.

In specialised farming, a farmer concentrates on a single enterprise, such as the production of market garden crops or broiler birds. In this system, the farmer needs specialised training and knowledge as well as specialised tools and equipment. As a result, it is intensive farming and producing abundantly and more economically.

Remember these

Extensive farming	Farming done on an expansive land area but with little inputs of capital and skilled labour.
Farming system	Method of farming characterised by certain particular features.
Intensive farming	Farming designed to bring high returns in a short period of time, but on limited land area.
Mixed farming	System of farming in which crops are grown and animals are reared on the same farm.
Natural resources	Those elements of nature which satisfy the needs of people.
Organic manures	Manures derived from the remains of plants and animals.
Plantation	Several hectares of land cultivated with only one main crop.
Shifting cultivation	System of farming in which virgin forest is cleared by slashing and burning and planted with short-term crops. With decline in crop yield the farmer shifts to another forested area and continues with the slash and burn practice.
Skilled labour	Labour derived from persons with training in special skills.
Subsistence farming	Farming done in one's spare time and leisure hours only to supplement one's earnings and the family's food requirements.

Practical activities

1 Look at a mixed farm in your community:

   a Make a list of the crops grown and the animals reared on the farm.

   b Prepare a model to show the layout of the farm.

2 Observe a dairy farm *and* a vegetable farm on which market crops are grown.

   List the activities which take place on each farm.

3 Go on a field trip to a nearby plantation.

   a Identify the main crop grown.

   b Collect and label the raw materials and manufactured products of the farm.

Do these test exercises.

1 Select the best answer from the choices given.

a Which of these is NOT true about intensive dairy farming?

   A An expansive land area is an essential requirement.

   B The capital input is high.

   C Cattle houses must be well designed and properly constructed.

   D A high level of health and sanitation must be maintained.

b Which group is recognised as plantation crops?

   A papaw, water-melon, cucumber

   B cabbage, sweet pepper, cauliflower

   C yam, sett potato, cassava

   D sugar-cane, banana, coffee

c On a mixed farm:

   A a variety of crops are cultivated.

   B crops are grown and animals are reared.

   C different classes of livestock are reared.

   D a wide range of agricultural activities take place.

d The primitive practice of slashing and burning virgin forest lands for cultivation of short term crops is associated with

   A mixed farming.

   B subsistence farming.

   C shifting cultivation.

   D the plantation system.

e A farmer involved in subsistence farming operates the farm:

   (i) mainly with family labour.

   (ii) to supplement earnings and family food requirements.

   (iii) as the chief means of livelihood.

Which statements above are true about subsistence farming?

   A (i) and (ii) only.

   B (i) and (iii) only.

   C (ii) and (iii) only.

   D (i), (ii) and (iii) are all true.

2 Explain what you understand by:

a Adequate feeding standards.

b High capital input.

c Natural resources.

d Skilled labour.

e Secondary forest growth.

3 Say why:

a Shifting cultivation is not a desirable practice.

b Animals are important in mixed farming.

c Many people practise subsistence farming.

d Intensive farming needs high capital input.

4 Say how:

a Mixed farming maintains soil fertility.

b Shifting cultivation operates.

c Diseases are controlled on an intensively run animal farm.

d Plantation crops contribute to the economy of a country.

5 Differentiate between:

a Intensive and extensive farming systems.

b Mixed farming and subsistence farming.

c Plantation system and shifting cultivation.

6 Write a short paragraph about each of the following:

a Natural resources and human resources.

b Production on an economic scale.

c The importance of farming in a country.

d Intensive crop production.

8 Livestock production I – cattle

Lesson objectives

In this lesson you are going to learn about rearing cattle. On completing the lesson you should be able to:

1 Identify the body parts of cattle.

2 Name some breeds of cattle reared in the Caribbean.

3 State the characteristic features of the breeds of cattle named in (2) above.

4 State the purposes for which cattle are reared.

5 Identify beef type and dairy type cattle by their body features.

6 Give short descriptions of the different systems of cattle management.

7 Explain how herbage material is digested in the ruminant stomach.

8 Give a simple description of the care and management of dairy calves.

9 State the advantages of using artificial insemination on a cattle farm.

10 Name some pests and diseases of cattle and state the measures used for controlling them.

11 Make a list of the products and by-products obtained from the cattle industry.

The diagram on the next page shows you the body features of a cow. Observe a live cow and try to locate these body parts.

Types and breeds of cattle

Beef cattle

The beef animal is rather rectangular in shape. The hindquarters are deep and fleshy and the barrel is capacious. The milk yield is usually low. The animal gains weight rapidly and has a high killing out percentage.

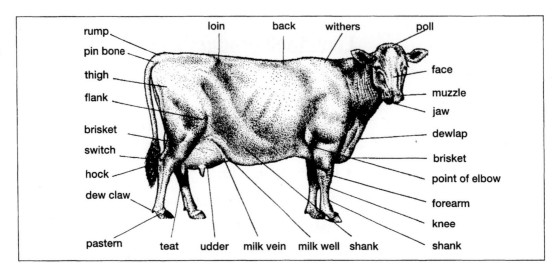

Beef is not yet produced on a very intensive scale in the Caribbean territories. Our locally produced beef is obtained from the bull-calves and culls of dairy herds and from small herds of beef cattle.

Jamaica Red

Zebu

Buffalypso

You will remember that the Jamaica Red and the Zebu are reared as beef cattle. However, crosses on an experimental scale have also been tried with tropical cattle and other breeds such as the Santa Gertrudis and the Charolais. These crosses have shown promising results. Good beef is also obtained from the Buffalypso, an animal bred in Trinidad especially for beef.

Dairy cattle

You will notice that the dairy cow, such as in the Holstein and Jamaica Hope breeds, is a wedge shaped animal. Its body is narrow to the front and broader towards the rear. The nostrils are wide, strong and well formed. There is a well developed chest and a deep barrel (abdomen). The udder is large; the teats are well formed, the milk veins are long and protruding whilst the milk wells are large enough for the finger to enter easily.

Dairy cows must also be able to thrive successfully under local conditions and give good milk yields over a long period of time. The animal must be docile and be quite willing to give her milk to the milker.

Holstein

Jamaica Hope

Holstein breed

The Holstein is a Canadian breed identified by its black and white coat. It is a large animal and gives very high milk yields. Pure bred Holsteins do not thrive very well under tropical conditions.

Jamaica Hope breed

The Jamaica Hope was produced by cross breeding the Jersey, a temperate breed, and the Sahiwal, a tropical breed native to India. The cross-breeding was done at the Hope Farms in Jamaica. The Jamaica Hope is noted for high quality milk and for high milk yields. It is well suited to Caribbean conditions.

Adaption of dairy cattle

Under very high temperatures, the animals suffer from heat stress. As a result there is a rise in body temperature, a decline in food intake, an increase in water consumption and a decrease in live-weight gain and in milk production.

The Zebu is heat tolerant. It utilises energy and allows productive processes to continue without the production of excessive amounts of heat. However, its milk production is poor and consequently not suitable for dairy purposes.

Holsteins and Jerseys give high milk yields but they are not heat tolerant and do not show resistance to tropical diseases. Do you think that they would perform as well in the Caribbean as they do in their home countries?

Temperate dairy cattle introduced into the Caribbean must be adapted for the local environment. This is done by cross-breeding and by good management practices. Their Holstein-Zebu offspring show some degree of heat tolerance and give good milk yields.

Care and management of cattle

Systems of management

Beef and dairy cattles could be reared intensively, extensively or on a semi-intensive scale. In an intensive system a large number of animals are reared in a limited space. High capital inputs are required. Houses are well designed and constructed and the level of feeding and sanitation is high.

In an extensive system the animals roam and graze over a large area with minimum care and management. There is very little capital input and skilled labour is not essential.

The semi-intensive system of management is used by the majority of cattle farmers in the Caribbean. In this system, the animals are put on pastures by day and brought into the pens at night. The bulk of their feed comes from pasture grasses and this is supplemented with rations.

Housing and equipment

Proper housing is essential especially in the intensive system of management. The building must be constructed to

Cattle pen, semi-intensive rearing

protect the animals from adverse weather conditions, to make them comfortable and to facilitate feeding, sanitation and ease of movement. The roof should be covered with corrugated aluminium sheets, and ventilation and light should be adequate. The floor should be concreted and there should be good drainage. Watering devices and feeding troughs should be installed.

External view of proper housing for cattle

Guinea grass, a useful fodder grass

Foods and feeding

You have learnt that the chief nutrients required by animals are carbohydrates, proteins, fats, vitamins, minerals, and water. These are essential for growth, milk production and good health.

Pasture and fodder grasses

Cattle are ruminants. They feed on pasture and fodder grasses, such as pangola, para, elephant, guinea and guatemala. Grasses should be fed while they are still green and succulent. At this stage they are most nutritious and easily digested. Legumes are rich in nitrogen and should be included in the pastures. Do you know that nitrogen is essential in the manufacture of body proteins?

A pasture

Dairy rations

Dairy rations are concentrated feeds with high energy and protein values. The type and quantity of ration needed depends upon the age of the animal and its state of production. For example, calves usually begin with a starter ration whilst heavy milkers require large quantities of lactation feeds. Fatteners near to slaughtering receive a finishing ration high in carbohydrate whereas dry or empty cattle receive little or no ration at all.

Mineral lick – a block containing essential minerals

Mineral licks

Minerals are needed for healthy growth and for the structure of bones and teeth. They are also essential for regulating body fluids and the activities of muscles and nerves. Large quantities of minerals are also found in milk. These minerals are supplied to the animal in the form of a salt block known as a **mineral lick**.

Maintenance and production rations

Cattles need adequate amounts of feed to maintain themselves and for the production of body weight, milk, and extra energy as in the case of working animals. A maintenance ration supplies the nutrients required to maintain the animal in a good state of health without adding extra live-weight or producing extra quantities of milk.

However, animals in production such as lactating cattles or fatteners need extra ration which is over and above the maintenance requirements, and this must be regarded as a production ration. Production rations are usually sold as commercial feeds, specially prepared for the type of production needed.

Digestion of grasses and other herbages

Cattle are ruminants. They feed chiefly on **herbage** and they have a complex stomach. Study the diagram below and try to recall the functions of the various parts of the digestive system of a ruminant animal.

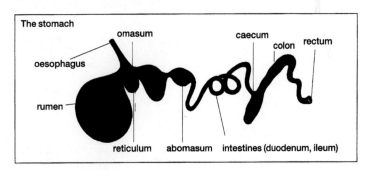

Ruminant digestive system

In Book 2 you learnt about the structural features of the ruminant stomach and the digestion of herbage material. You will remember that the rumen is the largest of the four compartments. Grasses and leaves eaten by the animal are stored in the rumen. During rumination the food is regurgitated, chewed with saliva and swallowed again.

Further breakdown of **cellulose** in the rumen takes place by means of bacterial activity. From the rumen the food enters the reticulum where it is mixed with liquid and ground further and passed on to the omasum. In the omasum the food is again ground and the liquids extracted. The food is then passed on to the abomasum where it is finally acted upon by the gastric juices. The contents of the abomasum is then passed on to the small and large intestines for digestion and absorption. The waste substances are passed out as excreta (urine and dung).

Breeding cattle

A **heifer** is ready for mating when she is about 11–13 months old. She should be selected from parents with the desirable characteristics and performance for the purpose for which the animal is to be reared. The animal should be strong, healthy, physically mature and weigh 300–350 kg. Breeding may be done naturally or by artificial insemination.

Natural breeding

In natural breeding the calf is taken to the bull for service. The bull must be strong, healthy, masculine in nature and possess the desired characteristics of either a beef type or dairy type animal. He should be physically mature and preferably in his second or third year of service. It is important to ensure that the bull is not too heavy (this will help to protect the heifer from injury during service).

Dairy bull (Holstein)

Artificial insemination (AI)

Artificial insemination is now practised in many of the Caribbean territories. The process involves the collection of semen and its insertion into the female reproductive tract during oestrus (or heat).

Semen is collected in an artificial vagina from which it is recovered, diluted and stored. The insertion of semen in the female tract is done by means of special syringes. The operation is a technical one and must be performed by trained inseminators.

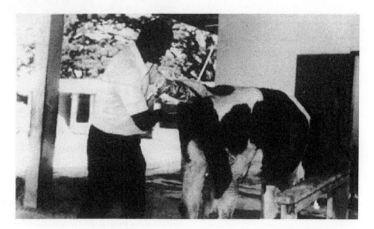

Artificial insemination: a trained insemi-nator inserting semen into the genital tract via the vulva of a cow on heat.

Cattle farmers prefer the use of artificial insemination to that of natural service as there are several advantages to be gained by this method. Cattles can be inseminated with semen collected from an outstanding bull in a far away district or country. The servicing of the animals can be better timed and often at a cheaper cost. The spread of diseases of the genital tract are minimised.

By means of artificial insemination, the farmer is better able to control the breeding programme so that a regular supply of beef or milk product can be obtained from the farm. As a result the farmer obtains a regular income from the farming enterprise.

Oestrus (or heat)

A cow should be mated at oestrus time (also known as the heat period). This period lasts for 12–28 hours and the **oestrous cycle** occurs every 21 days. She should be mated between the middle and the end of her heat period, that is, within the first 24 hour of oestrus. This is to ensure that conception takes place.

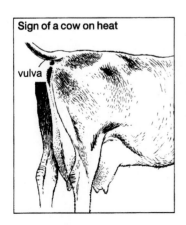

Sign of a cow on heat

vulva

A cow on heat has an abnormal behaviour. She is restless, her vulva is flushed and swollen and she allows herself to be mounted by other animals.

Pregnancy and parturition

A pregnant cow is one that is in young. The **pregnancy** period begins at conception and ends with parturition, that is, with the birth of the calf.

Pregnant cows

During the last 8–10 weeks of pregnancy, the fetus develops rapidly and makes heavy demands on the mother. The cow should have a constant supply of clean, fresh water and adequate amounts of dairy ration in her diet. This keeps her strong and healthy and enables her to give good milk yields in her next lactation.

About 5–7 days before **parturition**, the animal is brought into a calving pen. Litter or bedding is placed on the floor to keep her dry and warm and to facilitate easy cleaning of the pen. At parturition time there should be no disturbance. When the calf is born, it is dried and its mouth and nostrils cleaned. The umbilical cord, (navel string), is cut to a length of 10 cm from the calf's body and removed. The navel is then treated with a solution of iodine. An hour later the calf attempts to nurse. If it is weak, it should be assisted in its efforts to do so.

Assisting a calf to nurse

The afterbirth (the membrane enclosing the fetus in the mother's womb) is generally expelled within 24 hours. This must be removed and the soiled bedding replaced. The cow may not eat, but she should have a good supply of clean, fresh water. If difficulty arises during parturition, the assistance of a veterinary officer should be sought.

Rearing calves

Feeding

A calf gets colostrum for the first 2–3 days after birth. You will remember that colostrum is rich in proteins, vitamins and minerals. It is slightly laxative in nature and so aids the movement of the digestive tract. Colostrum also contains antibodies which protect the calf from diseases.

With beef animals, the calves are usually allowed to run along with their mothers and nurse freely. By the end of the third month the calves are gradually weaned and put on the pasture.

Bucket feeding a dairy calf

Age of calf (weeks)	Daily Requirements (in litres)		Other requirements	
	Colostrum and whole milk	Milk substitutes		
1	2.5–4.5	none	1	Provision of:
2	6–7	none	a	adequate supplies of pure fresh water;
3–5	4.5	4.25	b	mineral lick.
6–7	3.25	3.25	2	Introduced to:
8	2.25	2.25	a	cut grass and starter rations by week 3;
9	1.25	1.25	b	pasture during week 4.

Dairy calves are separated from their mothers when they are 2–3 days old and are fed from a bucket. The table on page 101 shows a feeding programme used in many dairy farms.

Housing of dairy calves

Look at this picture of a calf house. It is covered and well ventilated. The floor is concreted and there are wooden slats on it to keep the calf off the bare concrete.

The calf is kept in a calf-box: a blocked area about 1.5 m × 1 m with a feeding rack, a watering device and a stand for a mineral lick. Doors and passageways are located and constructed to facilitate ease of movement and to help maintain good sanitation practices.

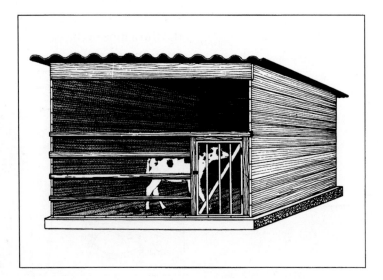

A well built single calf box

Other management practices

The farmer ensures that calves are vaccinated against diseases, such as anthrax and rabies. The calves are dehorned before they are 2 months old and dewormed at weaning time (3 months old). Bull calves that are not needed for breeding are castrated when they are 4–6 months old.

Pastures are provided with shade trees and a good supply of drinking water. Rotational grazing is essential as it helps to maintain good pastures and prevents the build-up of worm infestation and diseases.

Good pastures, with shade, for rotational grazing

Milk production

Look at this diagram of the internal structure of a cow's udder. Milk is secreted in the alveoli (milk secreting tissues) and taken through ducts to the gland cistern. From here the milk enters into the teat cistern and finds its way out through the teat canal under udder pressure or in the process of nursing or milking.

The foodmarkets require milk of high quality. To obtain this a farmer ensures that the cattle and stock handlers are healthy and free from disease. Strict sanitation in the milking programme is essential. The cows are thoroughly washed, the udders are cleansed with a bacterigent and the milker's hands are dried before milking. The first draw of

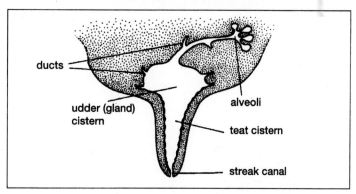

Internal structure of a cow's udder (only one of the quarters is shown)

milk is usually collected in a strip cup for observation. Milking machines, milk churns and storage containers are thoroughly washed and sterilised before they are used. On large farms the milk is also pasteurised. It is heated for 30 minutes at 60°C and then cooled, bottled and refrigerated.

Pests and diseases

You will recognise a healthy animal from its bright and alert look and from its shiny coat. It is active, it feeds vigorously and its droppings are firm and solid. However, the health of our cattle may be affected by several pests and diseases. Four are discussed below, but other important diseases are anthrax, foot-and-mouth, bovine tuberculosis, foot-rot, milk fever and cattle scours.

Roundworm of the intestines

The roundworm is the most common intestinal worm found in cattle. It punctures and extracts its food supply from the intestinal walls. An infested animal has a dull, ruffled coat. It has a poor appetite and fails to put on weight. Very often there is a scour with an intolerable stench.

The egg of the worm is passed out of the intestines to the outside by means of the faeces. Soon the egg develops into the infective stage and if swallowed by a healthy animal, infestation begins. The young worm is released from the egg in the animal's stomach and finds its way to the intestines where it settles and continues to live and feed.

Healthy animals can be protected from worm infestation by good pasture management. Pastures should be rotated regularly. Where calves and adult cattle share the same pastures, the calves should be put on the pastures before the adult animals. Sick or infected pastures should be rested.

Cattle showing signs of infestation should be treated with vermicides, such as *Phenothiazine* and *Piperazine* once every 4–6 weeks.

Cattle ticks

The cattle tick is an external parasite. It feeds on the blood of the cattle and is responsible for spreading the diseases anaplasmosis and piroplasmosis (commonly known as tick fever). An animal suffering from tick fever is dull and listless. It loses its appetite, becomes anemic and develops a high temperature. In a severe case the animal may die.

You will observe in the diagram that the engorged female tick falls to the ground where she lays her eggs and then dies. When the eggs hatch, the seed ticks (baby ticks) climb on the grasses nearby and cluster at the grasstips. Soon,

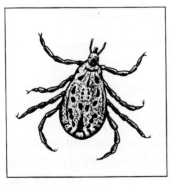

Cattle tick

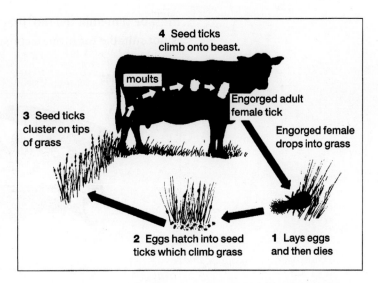

4 Seed ticks climb onto beast.

moults

3 Seed ticks cluster on tips of grass

Engorged adult female tick

Engorged female drops into grass

2 Eggs hatch into seed ticks which climb grass

1 Lays eggs and then dies

Life-cycle of the cattle tick

they are on the coat of another host that passes by. They feed on the host and gradually develop into the adult stage by moulting.

Ticks are controlled by spraying the infested animals with an acaricide, such as *Sevin*. The infected animal is sprayed under pressure with a mixture containing 28 g of *Sevin* to 4.5 l of water. After spraying, the animal is protected from the rain for at least 2 hours. Spraying is done once every 8–10 days.

Cattle mastitis

Mastitis is a disease of the udder. It is caused by bacteria which enter through the teat canal and destroy the milk-secreting tissues. The infected udder becomes red and inflamed. The cow suffers discomfort and immense pain. Milk from the infected udder is usually clotted, blood-stained and may have a bad smell.

Mastitis is best controlled by good milking practices and a proper standard of sanitation. The cow should be properly cleaned and the udder washed with disinfectant. A strip cup is used for collecting the first milk from the teats and infection is indicated by the presence of a milk clot. The udder should be stripped of all its milk.

An infected cow needs special treatment. The udder must be washed with warm water and a bacterigent. The udder should be stripped of all its milk and treated with an antibiotic inserted into the teat orifice. Cattle suffering from mastitis should not be milked with a milking machine. It

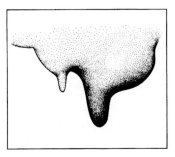

Mastitis infected udder

Strip cup

Milk clots

must be remembered too, that milk infected with mastitis is not suitable for human consumption.

Paralytic rabies

Vampire bat

Paralytic rabies is a virus disease which attacks cattle, many other domestic animals, and people. It is spread by the bite of animals infected by rabies. In Trinidad, the vampire bat is the chief carrier of the disease. An infected animal loses its appetite, finds difficulty in swallowing and salivates profusely. Paralysis sets in and the animal dies within 7–8 days.

Rabies is controlled by protection from bat bites and by vaccination with anti-rabies vaccines. Incidence of the disease should be reported to the veterinary officer or to the animal health department of your country.

Products of the cattle industry

As a result of the birth of new calves the farmer selects those that are needed for replacements or for expansion of the farm. The excess are sold as live animals to other farmers.

When these animals are slaughtered they are sold as fresh beef locally. Excess meat is either kept in cold storage for future use, exported to other countries or processed into such products as minced meats, burgers and corned beef.

Large quantities of fresh milk are consumed daily. Excess supplies of milk are manufactured into cream, butter, yoghurt, cheese and various types of canned and dried (powdered) milk. Milk is considered to be a perfect food and it is very desirable for people of all ages.

There are several other by-products of the cattle industry: hides are made into leather; the offal, bones and blood are used in the production of animal feeds and fertilisers;

excreta is decomposed to form organic manures; the horns are used for making small ornaments and the hooves are made into a glue.

Summary

Cattle are reared mainly for beef or for dairy products. Beef type cattle show distinct differences in body features from dairy type cattle. The major difference lies in the fact that beef animals tend to put on rapid body weight but their milk yield is low whereas dairy animals are high milk yielders.

The main breeds of beef cattle reared in the Caribbean are the Jamaica Red, the Zebu and more recently the Buffalypso, whereas the Jamaica Hope and the Holstein–Zebu crosses are reared for milk. Holstein–Zebu crosses are preferred to either the Holstein or the Zebu because they give higher milk yields than the Zebu and they are also better adapted to tropical conditions than the Holstein.

Cattle are reared intensively, extensively or on a semi-intensive system. Most farmers in the Caribbean operate on the semi-intensive system where the animals are put on pasture by day and brought into the pens at night. Proper housing is essential to protect the animals from adverse weather conditions and to make them comfortable. The house should be constructed to facilitate feeding, watering, sanitation and ease of movements.

Cattle obtain their nutrient supplies from pasture and fodder grasses supplemented by commercial rations. These feeds must meet the maintenance and production needs of the animals. The former is required only to maintain the animals in a good state of health whilst the latter is for the addition of extra weight or the production of milk. Cattle are ruminants: the stomach is complex and is adapted to digest pasture grasses and other herbage materials.

A heifer is bred when she is 11–13 months old, either naturally by taking the animal to the bull for service or by artificial insemination. Mating is usually done within the first 24 hour of oestrus to ensure that conception takes place.

Special care should be taken with pregnant animals. When the calf is born, it is allowed to nurse: this ensures that it receives the colostrum which is essential for the young animal. Subsequently, the calf is allowed to suckle and run along with its mother until it is weaned as with beef cattle, but a dairy calf is removed from its mother by the second or third day and put on a special feeding programme consisting of whole milk and milk substitute. The calf is provided with fresh water, starter ration, mineral lick and gradually introduced to grass. Other management practices include vaccination against diseases, dehorning, deworming and in the case of male animals, castration.

An animal in good health is bright, alert, active and possesses a shiny coat. Roundworms of the intestines, cattle ticks, cattle mastitis and paralytic rabies are studied. These parasitic infestations and ailments are usually controlled by vaccination, sanitation and the use of medication.

Cattle rearing provides a livelihood for many farmers. The industry supplies several products and by-products. These are broadly grouped as live animals for sale, meat and meat products, milk and milk products and by-products such as hides, organic manures, fertilisers and animal feeds.

Remember these

Artificial insemination (AI)	The process of inserting semen into the female reproductive tract during oestrus.
Cellulose	A carbohydrate material which forms the cell wall in plant cells.
Heifer	A female cattle that has not yet given birth to a calf.
Herbage	Plant material used as animal feed.
Lactation	Milk production.
Mineral lick	Salt block containing essential mineral elements.
Natural breeding	The system of breeding in which the female animal is brought to the male for service.
Oestrous cycle	The length of time between one heat period and the next.
Parturition	The act of giving birth.
Pregnancy	The period during which an animal is in young.

Practical activities

1 Visit either a beef or dairy farm and find out the following:
  a The breed or breeds of cattle reared.
  b Some characteristic features of the breed or breeds.
  c The system of management.
  d The types of fodder grasses and rations fed to the animals.
  e Is the farm operated by the farmer and family or by hired labour?hired labour?
2 Interview a dairy farmer and then write an account of 'A working day in the life of a dairy farmer'. Ensure that the correct sequence of events is maintained.

3 Carefully observe a calf house.

   a State the materials used for constructing the house.

   b List the devices installed in the building to facilitate feeding and watering; and the provisions made for the maintenance of health and sanitation of the animals.

4 Check the grocery shelves in your village. Prepare a list of:

   a Dairy products on sale.

   b Meat and meat products derived from cattle.

Do these test exercises

1 Select the best answer from the choices given.

  a The breed of cattle best suited for beef production is:

    A the Jamaica Hope

    B the Zebu

    C the Holstein

    D the Jersey

  b The Jamaica Hope was produced by cross breeding:

    A the Holstein and the Sahiwal

    B the Holstein and the Zebu

    C the Jersey and the Zebu

    D the Jersey and the Sahiwal

  c The part of the cattle stomach labelled 'P' is the:

    A omasum

    B rumen

    C reticulum

    D abomasum

  d A lactation ration is fed to an animal:

    A in her late pregnancy.

    B that was recently weaned.

    C in milk production.

    D fattened for slaughtering.

2 Explain what you understand by:

  a A heat tolerant animal.

  b Artificial insemination.

  c Holstein–Zebu crosses.

  d Succulent grass.

  e Trace elements.

3 Say why:

  a Offspring from Holstein-Zebu crosses are more heat tolerant than pure bred Holsteins.

  b Calves should be vaccinated.

  c Zebu cattles are not desirable on dairy farms.

  d Legumes are desirable in pastures.

  e Colostrum is important for calves.

4 Say how you would recognise:

  a A cow in good health.

  b A good dairy cow.

  c A worm infested calf.

  d A cow on heat.

5 Tell how:

  a You will attend to a newly born calf.

  b You will treat an udder that is infected with mastitis.

  c Milk is pasteurised.

  d Refrigeration prevents milk spoilage.

6 Write a short essay on one of the following.

  a Products of the cattle industry.

  b The production of high quality milk.

7 Write a short paragraph entitled 'The effect of heat stress on dairy cattle'.

9 Livestock production II – pigs

Lesson objectives

Some farmers rear pigs for their livelihood. In this lesson you are going to learn about rearing pigs. On completing this lesson you should be able to:

1 Identify the body parts of a pig.

2 Name some breeds of pigs reared in the Caribbean.

3 State the characteristic features of the breeds of pigs named in (2) above.

4 State the purposes for which pigs are reared.

5 Give short descriptions of the intensive and extensive systems of pig management.

6 List some fodder materials and rations fed to pigs.

7 Give a description of the care and management of a litter of piglets from birth to weaning.

8 State the physical features you will consider in selecting a pig for breeding.

9 Name some pests and diseases of pigs and state the measures used for controlling them.

10 Make a list of the products and by-products obtained from the pig industry.

Some livestock farmers rear pigs. If you visit a few pig farms in your country you will see several breeds of pigs. In order to describe them more fully make a study of the external features of the pig. Observe a pig carefully and locate the body parts shown in the picture below.

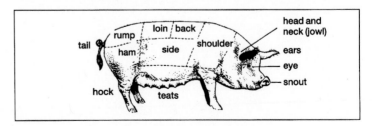

Parts of the body of a sow (female pig)

Breeds of pig

Do you remember what is meant by a **breed** of animal? It is a group or strain of animals with certain common characteristic traits or features. Some breeds of pigs reared in the Caribbean are the Large White, Large Black, Berkshire, Landrace, Hampshire and Tamworth.

Large White

Landrace

Large White

The Large White is a British breed. Each pig is large and white. A sow usually produces about 10 piglets per litter. The carcase is long and is best used for bacon production. In the Caribbean it is used as a porker pig (pork production) and is slaughtered at a weight of 63–68 kg.

Large Black

The large black breed are long, black pigs, with lop ears and good hams. They are hardy animals and graze extensively. The sows produce a large number of piglets to the litter and are good mothers. Farmers improve their local pigs by crossing them with the Large Black.

Berkshire

The Berkshire breed is noted for its rusty colour, erect ears, 6 white points on feet, nose and tail, its dish-face, broad carcase and the large quantity of muscle on its hind legs. Berkshire pigs mature early and are used for pork production.

Landrace

The Landrace breed is Danish in origin. The pigs are long, white skinned, have lop ears and are very prolific. Like Large White pigs, they are reared as porker pig and are slaughtered at about 63–68 kg in weight.

Systems of management and housing

Intensive system

Intensive pig rearing unit

Pigs are kept in a piggery which consists of a number of pens designed for accommodating as many pigs as possible within a limited space. Pens are concreted and provided with feeding and watering troughs. Just enough space is given to suit the kind of animal, its various stages of development, and the purpose for which it is reared, i.e. weaner, breeder or porker.

Intensive pig rearing requires adequate feeding standards, good sanitation measures, and proper control of pests and diseases. This system of management involves high capital cost, especially in the early stages of development.

Extensive system

The pigs are run out-of-doors or in a semi-covered yard. This extensive system involves low capital cost, but more skilled labour is needed. The cost of food may also be reduced, as the animals are allowed to graze or forage on young or succulent plants. A good rotational system of

Small pig houses

Pig foraging on pasture

Pig rearing on an extensive scale

Pig rearing on an extensive scale

grazing must be practised in order to avoid the build-up of pests and internal parasites.

Housing and equipment

Pigs need to be protected from hot sun, draughts, and cold air. Pens should be covered and well ventilated. The floor of the pen should be concreted, but it must not be too smooth. There should be adequate floor space, water and feeding troughs. Farrowing pens should be provided with farrowing rails and a creep feed area. The building should be designed to facilitate the washing of pens and the easy removal of dung. Good drainage and adequate water supply are essential.

Foods and feeding

Pigs are **omnivorous feeders**: they feed on both plant and animal products. Feeds must be well-balances and must meet the requirements of the age, the stage of development and the purpose for which the animals are reared.

Young and growing pigs need rations that are high in protein and mineral content, whereas breeding sows and boars need a well-balanced ration of carbohydrates, proteins, vitamins and mineral salts. Breeding animals should be kept in a fit condition and not allowed to become too fat, as this may result in breeding problems. For porker and bacon-type pigs, the feed must be regulated to meet the requirements of good carcase quality.

Herbage and vegetable materials

Growing pigs need about 5–6 kg of green materials in their daily diet. Green materials are a good source of vitamin and mineral supplies. Potato slips, spinach, patchoi, remains of legume crops, succulent grasses such as water grass, and elephant and para grass in their young stages of growth are good feeding materials. Hard fibrous grasses should be avoided as they are not easily digested. Do you know that the pig has a small simple stomach, similar to that of the rabbit or a human?

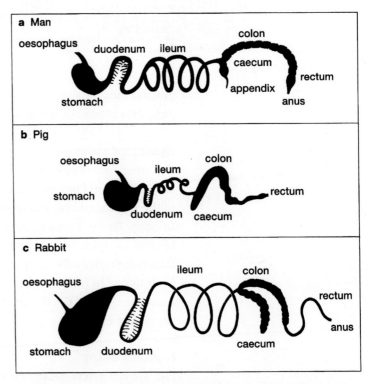

The simple stomach

Pigs also relish other vegetable matter such as the roots of cassava, sweet potatoes, yams, dasheen and arrowroot. Fruits and vegetables, such as banana, citrus, tomato, and pumpkin, may also be used as feeds.

Pig farmers who live near abattoirs or near fishing centres may feed the offal and other waste animal and fish products to their pigs. These products may also be processed to give meat and fish meals which are high in protein content. On dairy farms milk and milk by-products form valuable additions to the meals of young pigs.

Swills as feeds

Swills and left-over food materials and kitchen scraps from large institutions, such as hotels, boarding houses, and hospitals are good feeding materials, but they must be properly boiled before they are used as feeds.

Commercial feeds

Several types of commercial pig feed are available on the market. Some of these are fish meal, coconut meal, cotton seed meal, rice bran and wheat middlings. Any one of these feeds by itself is not adequate as a ration. Can you tell why? Would there be a proper balance of food nutrients?

Most farmers purchase commercially manufactured pig rations which contain a proper balance of carbohydrates, proteins, vitamins and minerals. Such rations are specially designed for pigs at their different stages of growth and development. The rations are generally in the pelleted form and are often known as creep-feed, pig starter and pig-finisher. Nursing mothers are given a special lactation ration.

Collecting swills

PIG STARTER

LACTATION PELLETS

PIG FINISHER

piglets on a starter ration

Selection of breeding pigs

Breeding pigs should be selected from good boars and sows. Selection must be based on the appearance of the animals, and on their performance records.

Appearance

Sow for breeding (Large Black)

Good breeding stock shows the following qualities:
1 A strong, straight top-line.
2 A well-muscled body with little fat.
3 Short, sound bones with strong pasterns.
4 Good width between the fore-legs.
5 Hams should be full and plump.
6 Breeding gilts should have at least 12 good teats, that are well placed.

Performance

The appearance of an animal is no indication of its ability to produce large, healthy thrifty litters. Breeding boars and sows should be selected from good mothers which produce an average of 8 piglets to the litter, and by weaning time, 8 weeks after birth, each piglet should weigh 15–18 kg.

Breeding

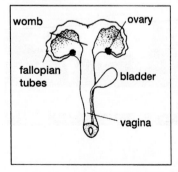

The reproductive organs of the sow

Boars and sows may be ready for breeding when they are 8–10 months old. They should be physically developed and weigh 102–113 kg.

Gilts or **sows** are mated when they show signs of heat. At this stage the vulva is swollen, reddish in appearance, and slime or mucus may be present. During heat (oestrus), ovulation takes place: ova or eggs are shed from the ovaries into the oviducts. The picture at the left shows you the reproductive organs of the sow. Study it carefully, it will help you to understand more about the breeding of sow.

Mating a sow during her heat period should result in fertilisation and pregnancy. The heat period in a sow lasts 2–3 days, and the oestrous cycle (the time between one heat period and the next) occurs every 21 days. The period from the time of conception to farrowing is 116–120 days.

Care and management of pregnant pigs

Pregnant sows should be kept in individual pens. They should be provided with adequate supplies of water and green materials, and given a suitable ration containing about 14–15% protein. A pregnant sow should get about 2–3 kg of commercial feeds daily, that is, about 1.75% of its body weight. The animal should be fed twice a day, once in the morning and once in the afternoon.

The sow should be taken to the farrowing pen at least one week before she farrows. She should be given dry litter with which to build a nest, but no food should be given on the days before or after farrowing. She should be given a good supply of fresh water. On the second day after farrowing the sow should be given about two handfuls of food, which is gradually increased each day until she is on full feed, at 10–14 days after farrowing. By this time she should be getting about 4–5 kg of feed (lactation pellets) daily.

Care of young piglets from birth to weaning stage

A good sow farrows from 8–12 piglets. Farrowing lasts for up to 12 hours. During this time the sow should not be disturbed.

The piglets are born with a thin membrane covering their bodies. This membrane splits soon after birth. It must be removed and the piglets should be dried. Long navel cords must be cut at 7–10 cm from the body and painted with iodine. The piglets should be allowed to suckle soon after

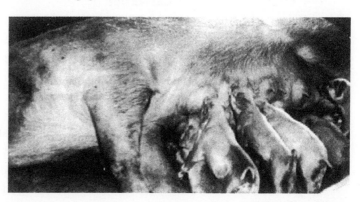

Sow suckling her litter

birth. It is essential that the young pigs get the first milk or colostrum from their mother as this is high in proteins and contains antibodies which help to immunise the piglets against diseases.

The pen must be kept as dry as possible. The expelled after-birth should be removed, or it will be eaten by the mother.

The body temperature of the piglets tend to drop for the first 30 minutes after birth. Under cold conditions they may die. The temperature of the pen should be maintained between 31°C and 32°C for the first 2 days and then gradually returned to normal temperature. Many farmers use infra-red lights in the pens during the first 2–3 weeks of the pig's life.

Creep feeding

Piglets should be given **creep feed** when they are 6–7 days old. The feed must be protected from the mother, but must be within reach of the piglets.

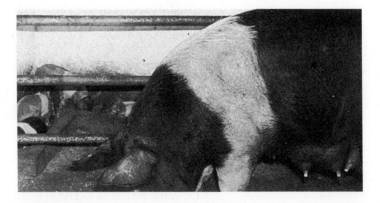

Creep feed for piglets

Castration

Male piglets that will not be used for breeding should be castrated when they are about 5–6 weeks old. This makes the management of boars easier and prevents breeding in undesirable boars.

Pig marking

Piglets selected for breeding should be marked so that they can be recognised easily, and their performance can be recorded. Markings are best done by tattooing the skin or by punching and notching the ears.

The picture on this page shows you a system of ear marking. Now try to find out what is the number of piglets A, B, and C in these pictures.

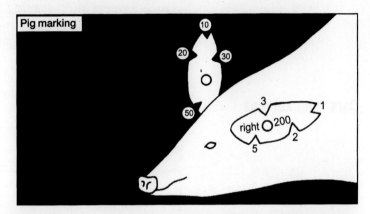

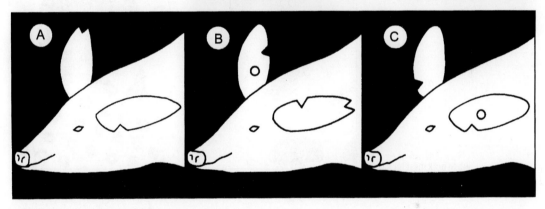

Find out what is the number of piglets A, B and C

Immunisation

What is immunisation? Why are animals immunised?

Immunisation is the treatment with chemicals or vaccines against the possibility of catching certain diseases. Swine fever and swine erysipelas are two common diseases which cause sudden death and a heavy loss of pigs on many farms. Piglets are inoculated against these diseases when they are 6–8 weeks old.

Weaning

Piglets are weaned when they are about 8 weeks old. The process should be gradual. The mother is first removed for some hours, then for a day or two, and then completely. Weaned piglets should be kept warm. They may suffer from weaning scours. If this occurs they should be treated with an antibiotic. High or over-feeding should be avoided.

During weaning, the feed of the sow should be reduced. This helps to dry her off (stop the production of milk) and bring her back on heat at an earlier date.

At 2–3 weeks after weaning, the piglets may be sold as **weaners** or selected for breeding purposes. Most farmers, however, continue to rear their pigs for pork production.

Care of porker pigs

In the Caribbean, pigs are generally reared for pork production. The animals are slaughtered when they are 5½ to 6 months old, with an approximate live-weight of 62–67 kilograms.

Fresh pork meat for sale

Porker pigs are kept in community pens in groups of 3–4 to a pen. The pigs are fed on a special fattening ration and should be given adequate supplies of clean drinking water. Good sanitation should be ensured and maintained on the farm.

Pigs should be dewormed every 3–4 months. Intestinal worms puncture the walls of the intestine and feed on the blood of the animal. The animal becomes unhealthy and unthrifty.

Care and management of boars

Breeding boars should be separated when they are four months old. They should be fed on a well-balanced ration and housed in a pen with adequate moving space. An open run for exercise is also desirable.

A breeding boar

The boar should not be kept too far away from the rest of the animals, as this tends to make him vicious and ferocious. A boar can begin service when he is 7½ to 8 months old.

The prevention and control of diseases and parasites

Young and adult pigs are attacked by several diseases and parasites. These cause unthriftiness and often lead to death.

Piglet anaemia

Young pigs confined to pens develop anaemia. This condition results from a lack of iron in the blood. To prevent this, farmers give iron inoculations when the piglets are 3–4 weeks old. Mineral licks or painting the teats of the mother with ferrous sulphate solution are also very helpful. Some farmers put clumps of clean soil in the pens. This helps because the soil contains traces of iron and other mineral elements.

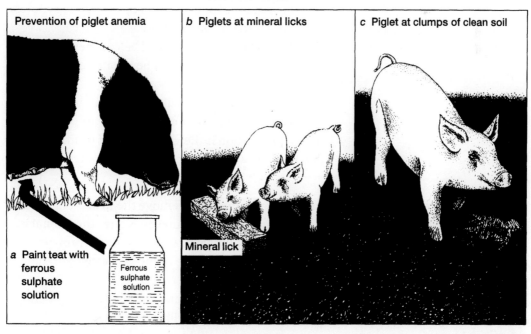

Prevention of piglet anemia

a Paint teat with ferrous sulphate solution

Ferrous sulphate solution

b Piglets at mineral licks

Mineral lick

c Piglet at clumps of clean soil

Scouring (diarrhoea)

Scouring or diarrhoea may occur in piglets at weaning time. It is accompanied by unthriftiness and a loss of weight. The disease may be caused by bacteria, or by nutritional deficiencies, overfeeding, or unfavourable environmental conditions.

Scouring is generally controlled by careful feeding. Piglets should be given nutritious feeds that are easily digested. Good sanitation is absolutely essential.

Hog cholera (swine fever)

Hog cholera is caused by a virus. It is both contagious and infectious, that is, the disease organism could be spread by contact or it may enter the body by means of air, water, or food. The disease is characterised by high fever and perhaps sudden death.

Can hog cholera be cured? So far, there is no effective treatment for the disease and affected animals are destroyed and buried.

Control measures

Hog cholera is a notifiable disease: that is, its incidence must be reported to the agricultural officer, the health department, or the police department. The recommended preventative measures are:

1 Avoid movement of animals or people from hog cholera infected areas to non-infected areas.
2 All swills must be properly boiled before they are fed to animals. Infected animals must be isolated and destroyed.
3 Infected pens, as well as feeding and watering utensils, should be disinfected before they are put into use again.
4 The best prevention is the vaccination of healthy pigs when they are about six or seven weeks old.

Dressed carcase and killing percentage

To dress a carcase means to remove the head, tongue, kidneys, heart, liver, hair, and intestines after the animal is slaughtered. The killing percentage is the percentage weight of the dressed carcase to the live-weight of the animal.

Now study the following calculations. They will help you to understand more about killing percentages.

Problem: A live porker weighs 63.6 kg and its dressed carcase weighs 47.7 kg. What is the killing percentage?

Solution:

Weight of live animal = 63.6 kg

Weight of dressed carcase = 47.7 kg

$$\text{Killing percentage} = \frac{\text{weight of dressed carcase}}{\text{weight of live animal}} \times \frac{100}{1}$$

$$= \frac{47.7}{63.6} \times \frac{100}{1} = 75 \text{ per cent}$$

At 75 per cent the killing percentage is considered very satisfactory.

Products of the pig industry

You will remember that pigs are reared mainly for meat or for use as breeding animals.

Live animals for sale

Many farmers produce live piglets only. Soon after weaning, the farmer selects the animals that he wants for his farm to continue with his breeding programme. The remaining piglets are sold as porker pigs or as animals for breeding.

Meat and meat products

The dressed carcase of the pig is made into special cuts and sold as fresh pork in the market place, groceries and meat shops.

Excess supplies are kept in cold storage for future use or exported to other countries. There are also several manufactured meat products from the pig. The most popular ones are ham, bacon, sausages, hot dogs, burgers and pickled meats.

Other by-products

The main by-products of the pig industry are pig manure derived from the excreta of the animals and the manufacture of fertilisers from the offal and other waste parts of the slaughtered animal.

Summary

Pigs are reared mainly for meat or for breeding purposes. Among the many breeds of pigs found in the Caribbean, the Large White, Landrace, Large Black, Berkshire and Hampshire are the most popular.

Pigs may be reared intensively or extensively. The former system of management is practised where space is limited and the latter where space is available but capital inputs are generally low. Under the intensive system of management, housing is very important. Houses should be constructed to keep the animals comfortable and to facilitate feeding, watering, sanitation and ease of movement.

The pig is an omnivorous feeder. Its diet must be well balanced to meet the requirements of age, stage of development and the purpose for which it is reared. Its feed consists mainly of succulent herbs, rations and swills.

Pigs for breeding are selected mainly on their appearance and on their performance records. Boars and sows are ready for breeding when they are about 8–10 months old and must be at a good stage of physical development. During pregnancy the sow should have adequate supplies of feed and water. At farrowing time the farmer must be nearby to attend to the new born piglets. Soon after birth, the piglets are cleaned and dried, their navel cords cut and treated with iodine solution, and are allowed to suckle their mother. Subsequent care and management include creep feeding, castration of male piglets, pig marking, immunisation and deworming. The piglets are weaned when they are about 8 weeks old.

Pigs are attacked by several diseases and parasites. The major ones considered in this lesson are piglet anaemia, scouring and hog cholera. These ailments and parasitic problems are usually controlled by good feeding and sanitation practices, immunisation and the use of medication.

The main products of the pig industry are fresh pork or meat for the markets and other meat products such as ham, bacon, sausages, burgers and pickled meats. However, some farmers concentrate on live animals for sale as breeders or porkers. The by-products are organic manures and fertilisers manufactured from the offal and other waste parts of the slaughtered animal.

Remember these

Anaemia	The condition resulting from a lack of iron in the blood.
Breed	A group or strain of animals with certain common characteristic traits or features.
Creep feed	A ration or commercial feed given to piglets when they are about six or seven days old.

Gilt	A female pig that has not yet given birth to young piglets.
Omnivorous feeder	An organism that feeds on both animal and plant products.
Porkers	Pigs reared for meat, that is, for pork.
Sow	A female pig that has already given birth to young piglets.
Swills	Left-over food materials.
Weaner	A piglet that has been recently weaned from its mother.

Practical activities

1 Observe a pig carefully.
  a Identify the body parts of the pig shown in the picture on page 110.
  b Draw a pig and label the body parts.
2 Visit a nearby pig farm.
  a Identify the breeds of pigs on the farm.
  b State the characteristic features of the breeds of pigs you identified.
3 Your teacher will organise a field trip to some pig farms in your village.
  a Collect and label specimens of succulent fodder material and rations fed to the pigs.
  b Carefully observe a farrowing pen and then write a short description of the pen under the following headings: construction material; size of pen; equipment and the purposes they serve; and sanitation facilities.

Do these test exercises

1 Select the best answer from the choices given.

a Which breed of pig is of Danish origin:
   A The Berkshire
   B The Large White
   C The Landrace
   D The Hampshire

b Pigs should be fed on succulent fodder material because:
   A its moisture content is high.
   B it is easy to chew.
   C pigs are omnivorous animals.
   D pigs have a simple stomach.

c Piglet anaemia is caused by a deficiency in:
   A calcium
   B iron
   C sodium
   D magnesium

d The pregnancy period of a pig is between:
   A 96 to 104 days
   B 105 to 110 days
   C 112 to 115 days
   D 116 to 120 days

e A contagious disease is one in which the disease organism is spread by means of:
   A air
   B water
   C food
   D contact

2 What do you understand by:

a A breed of animals.
b Intensive pig rearing.
c The pig is an omnivorous feeder.
d Dressed carcase.
e A notifiable disease.
f Community pens.
g Creep feeding.

3 Describe how:

a A farmer weans a litter of pigs.
b You know when a sow is on heat.
c You will attend to a litter of pigs within the first 2–3 hours after their birth.
d A farmer prevents piglets from developing anaemia.

4 Give good reasons for:

a Marking or numbering piglets.
b Reducing the amount of ration given to a sow when her piglets are weaned.
c Feeding colostrum to piglets.

5 The killing percentage of a porker pig is 74% and the dressed carcase is sold at $2.20 per kg. Calculate the income from 12 porker pigs of average weight 60 kg. What profit would the farmer make on those pigs if 70% of the income is expended on inputs of feed, labour and medications?

10

Forestry and fishery in the Caribbean

Lesson objectives

In this lesson you are going to learn about the forestry and the fishing industries in the Caribbean. On completing this lesson you should be able to:

1 Discuss the importance of forestry and fishery to a country.

2 Explain the concepts of natural and cultivated forests.

3 Identify the ornamental trees and shrubs in your home and school compounds.

4 State the functions of a forester.

5 Identify the external features of a fish.

6 Identify some freshwater and salt-water fishes.

7 Give a simple description of the food and energy cycle in water.

8 List the fishing gears and equipment needed for coastal and deep sea fishing.

9 Name and describe some methods of coastal and deep sea fishing.

10 List some products obtained from the forest and the fishing industries.

11 Discuss some of the environmental problems associated with the forest and the fishing industries.

12 State the actions taken to protect and preserve forestry and fishery in the Caribbean.

13 State some safety measures relating to the forestry and fishery industries.

Do you know that the forest and the sea are two great natural resources?

Forestry

You will remember that the forest provides raw materials for human and industrial use. It also assists in the conservation and maintenance of soil fertility and in the storage and control of soil water.

Evergreen trees of the natural forest

Natural forests

The natural forests of the Caribbean territories consist chiefly of tall **evergreen trees**. On the stems and branches of these trees are found orchids, creepers and lianes of various types. The undergrowth is usually very thick. This type of vegetation predominates because the Caribbean is within the tropics where high temperatures and rainfall prevail almost the whole year through.

Cultivated forests

Teak is a sub-tropical forest tree. However, it is well adapted to the soils and climatic conditions of the Caribbean. You will notice that the teak sheds its leaves during the dry months of the year. This is a natural device adopted by the plant to reduce transpiration and so conserve its water supply to withstand the dry spell.

Caribbean pine is a useful forest tree. Small plantations of it can be seen in some parts of the countryside. This tree was introduced within the last 40–45 years and the plantations you see are almost ready for harvesting. The Caribbean pine shows great potential as a tree crop.

Young teak trees

Caribbean Pine trees

However, the period from planting to maturity is very long.

The effect and uses of forests

Conservation and control of soil water

You probably know that rainfall is higher in forested areas because the moisture laden winds are forced to rise to cooler regions. Condensation and cloud formation take place and rainfall results.

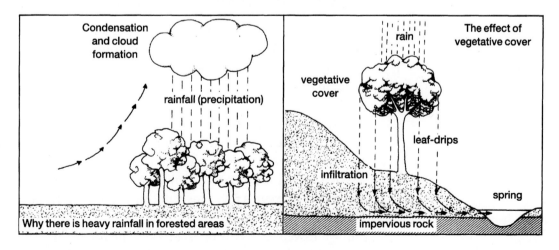

The vegetative cover of forest trees traps the raindrops and redistributes them, thus avoiding the torrential action of heavy downpours. Water infiltrates into the soil to feed the springs and rivers and to increase the supply of soil water. In this way the vegetative cover of forest trees reduces the incidence of flooding and the silting of roadways.

Improvement of soil fertility

You will remember that trees and vegetative cover crops protect and conserve the soil. You also know that the foliage of trees intercepts the raindrops and reduces splash erosion whilst the decomposition of leaf-litter adds organic matter to the soil, increases its water holding capacity and reduces run off.

The roots of trees bind soil particles and prevent the washing away of surface soil. When the trees die, the roots

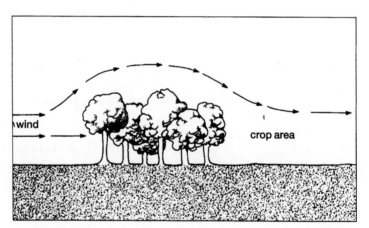

The forest acts as a wind barrier

decay to increase the organic content of the soil to greater depths. The pore spaces and channels left behind increase soil aeration and improve the movement and drainage of water in the soil.

Alteration of climate

Have you made a journey through a forest? Is it as hot in the forest as it is in the open sunshine? You will observe that it is cool in the forest. The foliage of the trees absorbs and reflects the sun's rays thus reducing the heat and modifying the temperature.

In windswept areas the forest acts as wind barrier. It reduces the velocity of the wind and forces it upward and around. This minimises wind erosion, prevents damage to tree crops and the loss of flowers and fruit.

You will remember too, that the forest attracts rainfall, so that most tropical forests are usually damp and wet.

Forest trees such as cedar, cypre and mahogany are sometimes planted to provide shade in cocoa, coffee and banana plantations. On maturity these trees may be harvested and used as timber for lumber.

Some other ways in which forests are useful

The forest is useful in several other ways. It provides employment for people engaged in the timber and lumber industries and the sale of forest trees is a source of revenue to the government. It must be remembered, too, that the forest is the natural home of many species of birds and wild animals and hence an avenue of sports and recreation for hunters and bird watchers. The fruits of some forest trees are edible and are used as food, whilst the many vines and lianes are sought by people in the art and craft trades. The forest also helps to improve our environment. Some trees have gorgeous flowers and are used for beautifying our lawns and parks. Others have thick evergreen foliage which filters the air and reduces atmospheric pollution. The dense foliage of trees also acts as sound barriers in a world that is filled with noises.

The diagram below shows you the variety of products which can be obtained from trees. Study it carefully and then indicate the products which are obtained from the

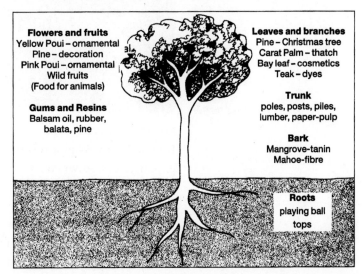

Products from forest trees

following trees: balata; bay leaf; teak; mangrove; mahoe; and pine.

Now investigate and find out the uses of the following forest trees: mora; greenheart; purple heart; crappo; cypre; jereton; bois flot; and palmiste.

Environmental problems associated with forestry

Heavy demands have been made on our indigenous forest over the last three decades. The accelerated house building programmes have led to the indiscriminate harvesting of useful forest trees. As a result, several environmental problems occur. For example, changes in weather conditions, loss of wild life and recreational facilities, a rise in atmospheric pollution and the exposure of the land. The last factor is responsible for erosion, land slides, flooding and the silting of drains and waterways.

Protecting our forests

The forest must be protected and maintained for future generations. This is achieved by the establishment of **forest reserves** and by the implementation of **reforestation programmes** by foresters who have been specially trained to do these jobs.

Boundary of a forest reserve

Forest reserves

Do you know what forest reserves are? They are large expanses of Crown lands or private lands set aside for the protection and promotion of the forest industry.

Reforestation programmes

Look at the forest industry in your own country and observe the reforestation programmes in operation.

Reforestation programmes are needed to maintain regular supplies of valuable woods. Forest plantations are established systematically from time to time and seedlings of high quality **indigenous forest** trees are planted in our forest reserves and on the mountain slopes. Experimental work and observations are conducted to determine the suitability and adaptability of new types of forest trees that could be introduced into the country.

The forester and his duties

This picture shows you some **foresters**. These officers are trained in the care and management of forest trees. They assist in implementing forest programmes and they ensure that the laws and regulations governing the forest are maintained.

Foresters are also responsible for the controlled harvesting of forest trees, for the preservation of the wildlife of the country and for the protection of the forest against such incidences as disease and bush fire.

Foresters care for forest trees

Fishing

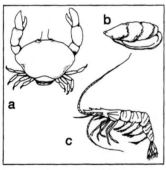

Think of the many ways in which our seas, swamps and rivers are used. They are used by thousands of people for recreational activities and they are exploited in the quest for food and raw materials for industry.

These pictures show you some water creatures caught by people and used as food. Identify them.

Among the many water creatures we eat, fish is caught and used in the greatest abundance. Fish are a good source of proteins and vitamins and supply the minerals, especially calcium and iodine.

The former is essential in the structure of bones and teeth whilst the absence of the latter may lead to the development of goitre, a disease of the thyroid gland.

Fish in our waters

There are several types of freshwater and salt-water fish. You may obtain them from the fish markets or from fish vendors on the wayside in the country areas. The following pictures show you some fish that are considered delicacies.

Goitre in man

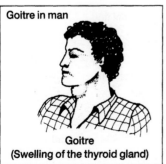

Goitre
(Swelling of the thyroid gland)

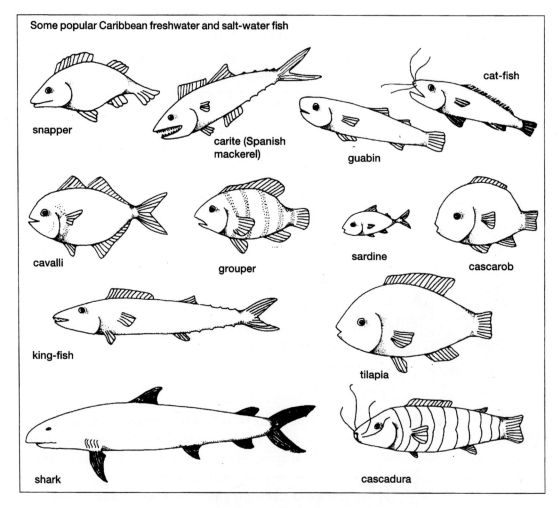

Some popular Caribbean freshwater and salt-water fish

snapper

carite (Spanish mackerel)

guabin

cat-fish

cavalli

grouper

sardine

cascarob

king-fish

tilapia

shark

cascadura

Now try to find out:

1 Which of these fish are freshwater ones and which are salt-water ones?

2 How these fishes differ from each other.

The features of a tilapia fish

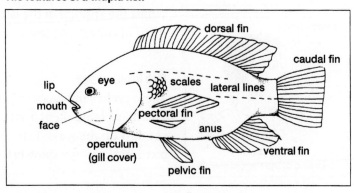

External features of a fish (tilapia)

The diagram on page 134 shows the external features of a tilapia fish. Try to identify and locate these features.

You have probably noticed that the carite and the kingfish have smooth bodies whilst the grouper and the snapper are scaly. You will observe, too, that the kingfish is bony whereas the shark is cartilaginous. Fish breathe by gills and obtain their oxygen supply from the waters in which they live.

In their feeding habits, the cascarob and the tilapia are herbivorous: they feed on algae, diatoms and water-weeds. The guabin, however, is carnivorous: it devours and feeds on smaller fish and other water creatures.

The tails and fins of fish assist them in their movements. The fish are propelled forward or directed to the right or to the left by means of their tails and other body muscles. Their pectoral, dorsal and pelvic fins stabilise and enable them to suspend themselves or move upward and downward in the water.

The food and energy cycle in a water environment

Fish and other water creatures obtain their food and energy supplies from the environment in which they live. Make a careful study of the food and energy cycle shown below and try to answer the questions which follow:

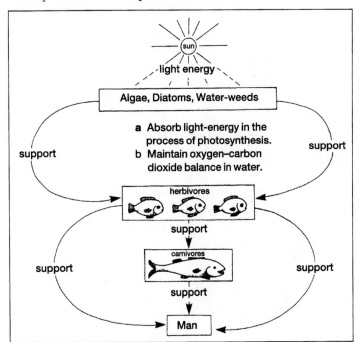

The food and energy cycle in water

1 From what source do water-weeds, algae and diatoms obtain their energy supply?
2 Why are these organisms able to carry out the process of photosynthesis?
3 How do herbivores obtain their food?
4 On what do carnivores feed?
5 How do herbivores and carnivores support humans?
6 How is the balance of oxygen and carbon dioxide maintained in a fish pond?

Fishing in rivers and swamps

Do you fish with hooks and baits or do you use a fish-net? Do you dive and try to catch the fish with your hands?

River fishing with a baited hook on a line

People who fish in the rivers and swamps do so with a baited hook or they may cast nets. It is not unusual to see fishermen diving into the waters and catching live fish with their hands.

Rearing fish in ponds and lakes

Experimental work has been done in the rearing of tilapia fish (*Tilapia mossambica*) in artificially constructed ponds and lakes. To rear good quality fish, it is essential that the pond is 1.5–2 m in depth and not be overstocked. It is also necessary to fertilise the ponds and to feed the fish periodically. If eels are present they should be destroyed as they feed upon the fish that are reared.

Tilapia is introduced into the swamps and rivers around. They thrive better and grow larger in these environments than in the ponds. Can you tell why?

The picture following shows you a wayside fish vendor with strings of tilapia for sale. These fish are now eaten extensively by many of our local inhabitants.

Fish pond

Wayside fish vendors

Coastal and deep-sea fishing

More people are engaged in fishing in the sea than in the swamps and rivers. They may fish along the coastline or far out into the seas. People who fish along the coast use small sailing boats or motor-boats. Sometimes, they fish with primitive weapons such as lances and harpoons, but they commonly use seines, lines with baited hooks, and fish traps to capture their prey.

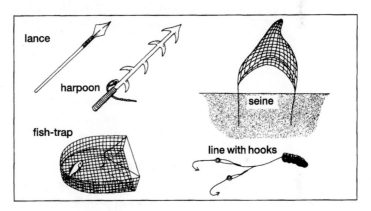

Some types of fishing gear

Deep-sea fishing

Trawler

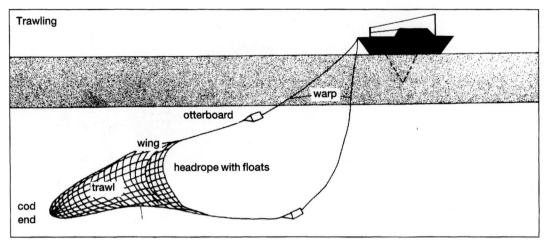

Trawlers are used for fishing far out at sea. These are large boats equipped with fishing gear and refrigeration units. They stay out at sea for as long as 10 to 12 days before they return to shore. A conical net (a trawl) is dragged slowly over the sea-bed. The mouth of the trawl is kept open by otter-boards. The trawling speed (2.5 knots) must be just sufficient to allow the trawl to keep to the bottom of the sea and to prevent the fish from escaping out of the net.

Do you think that this method of fishing could cause damage to the vegetation on the sea-bed?

Other methods of sea fishing are long-lining, trolling and drift-netting.

Fishing and industry

The fishing industry provides employment for a great number of people. You will observe, too, that there are several other industries and recreational activities associated with fishing or with our swamps and seas. Study the chart on this page. It tells you about these industries. You will learn more about them in your class discussion.

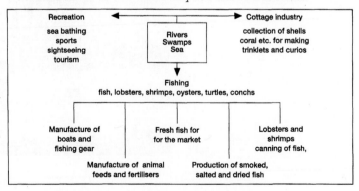

Environmental problems associated with the fishing industry

Our marine environment is highly endangered by the fishing industry and by offshore drilling activities.

Some fishermen are not selective about the fish they catch in a haul and so valuable young fish are destroyed. In the process of trawling the vegetation on the sea-bed is disturbed ultimately leading to a shortage of feeding materials for fish and other marine animals. From offshore drilling, there are occasional spills of oil slicks in the waters around. This substance is injurious to both the flora and fauna of the sea.

How the fishing industry is protected

Every effort is made to protect and perpetuate the fishing industry. Fishermen are given training in navigation, the use of fishing gear, fishing methods and in the proper way of handling and storing their catches. Fishing depots with refrigeration units are set up in the fishing districts, whilst financial and technical assistance are given by some governments for the establishment of canneries.

Laws are made to control **fishing limits**. These are boundaries off the coastline where foreigners cannot fish. Fishing limits vary from country to country and may extend from a distance of 3 to 12 miles or even more.

For some species such as the turtle, there is a **closed season** when it is an offence to catch them. This closed season usually coincides with their egg laying period.

In the case of inland fishing, farmers are often given financial assistance to construct fishponds. They are also given fish to stock the ponds and technical guidance in the care and management of the fish. Experimental work on the rearing of local fish species and freshwater prawns is also in progress.

Summary

The forest and the sea are two great natural resources. The former supplies raw materials for human and industrial use and the latter provides protein rich foods for people.

Forests may be natural or cultivated. The natural forests are indigenous to the Caribbean and are characterised by tall evergreen trees with thick undergrowth. The cultivated forest trees are mainly teak and Caribbean pine.

Forests are useful in several ways. They provide timber for the lumber industry, employment for people and a source of revenue to the government. Among the other useful purposes served by the forest are recreational facilities, materials for the craft industry and ornamental trees for beautifying our environment.

The need for timber and lumber have made a heavy demand on the forest over the last three decades. Indiscriminate harvesting of forest trees have resulted in several environmental problems such as changes in the weather and the loss of wild life and recreational facilities. The land is also exposed to the elements and this is largely responsible for erosion, flooding and the silting of drains and water ways.

The forest is an important resource: it has to be protected and maintained for future generations. This is done by reforestation programmes, and ensuring that the forest is properly cared for and managed by trained foresters.

Fishing is done in rivers, swamps and ponds or in the waters of the seas around. However, the major parts of the fishing industry is associated with the sea.

Fishes are grouped as freshwater or salt-water fishes. They are specially adapted for life in a water environment as they breathe by gills and move by means of fins and tails. According to their feeding habits they are described as herbivores or carnivores.

Sea fishing takes place on the coastline or in the deep seas. In coastline fishing small fishing boats are used and fishing is done by hooks and seines or even by primitive devices such as lances, harpoons and fish traps. In deep sea fishing large trawlers with refrigeration units are used. A trawl is dragged on the sea bed for catching fish. This method might be good for the fisherman, but it is destructive to the vegetation on the sea bed.

The fishing industry provides employment for many people. The catch from rivers, swamps and seas is used as food and excess quantities are smoked or canned for future use. Other by-products of the fishing industry are fertilisers and animal feeds as well as curios and other items of interest produced in the cottage industries. Rivers and seas also provide opportunities for recreation, sports and sight seeing.

Among the problems associated with the marine environment are the destruction of useful young fishes by thoughtless fishermen, damage to the sea bed by trawlers and the presence of oil slicks from offshore drilling.

The fishing industry must be protected and perpetuated. This is achieved by giving fishermen training in navigation; by establishing fishing depots, refrigeration units and canneries; making legislation and its enforcement in relation to fishing limits and the preservation of certain species of fishes and marine animals; and giving financial and technical assistance to people involved in the fishing industry.

Remember these

Closed season A particular period of time when its an offence to catch certain types of wild animals.

Cottage industry The production of small items of trade by the family members of a home.

Evergreen trees Trees having green leaves all the year round.

Fauna The animals of a region.

Fishing limits Boundaries off the coastline where foreigners cannot fish.

Flora The plants of a region.

Foresters Officers with specialised training in the care and management of forests.

Forest reserve A large expanse of Crown lands or private lands set aside for the protection and promotion of the forest industry.

Indigenous forests Forests belonging naturally to the area where they happen to exist.

Reforestation programmes The systematic establishment of forests plantations.

Practical activities

1 Visit a nearby sawmill or lumber yard and collect specimens of lumber material derived from local forest trees. Label the specimens and place them in your school laboratory.

2 Prepare a model to demonstrate the use of forest trees as a wind break to protect garden crops. Write a short paragraph explaining how the wind break operates.

3 Collect one of these fish: tilapia, cascarob, snapper.
   a Observe the fish carefully and identify the external features. Use the diagram on page 134 to help you.
   b Make a drawing of the fish identified in (a) and label the external features.

4 Collect or make your own specimens of the following fishing gear: harpoons and lances; lines with hooks; fish traps; a drift net.

Do these test exercises

1 Select the best answer from the choices given.

a A cartilaginous fish commonly used as food is the:

A carite

B bonito

C shark

D snapper

b The forward movement of a fish is initiated by the:

A gills

B tail

C head

D pectoral fins

c The natural forests of the Caribbean consist chiefly of tall evergreen trees because of:

A low temperatures and high rainfall.

B low temperatures and low rainfall.

C high temperatures and low rainfall.

D high temperatures and high rainfall.

d A good way to reduce erosion on steep hillsides is to:

A cultivate short term crops.

B grow tree crops.

C practise shifting cultivation.

D operate mixed farming.

2 Explain the following:

a Trees of ornamental value.

b Moisture-laden winds.

c Indigenous forest trees.

d Evergreen foliage.

e Closed season.

3 *Say how:*

a Forests help to reduce air pollution.

b The forests assist humans and animals with their food-supplies.

c The balance of oxygen and carbon dioxide in a pond is maintained.

d The forest attracts rainfall.

e Fish breathe and obtain their oxygen supply.

4 Differentiate between:

a Timber and lumber.

b Crown lands and private lands.

c Natural forests and cultivated forests.

d Herbivores and carnivores.

5 Write a short paragraph on each of the following:

a The functions of a forester.

b The need for seafoods in the diet of humans.

c The importance of forestry in my country.

d Deep sea fishing.

6 Identify two environmental problems associated with:

a the forest industry.

b the fishing industry.

7 List the measures taken to protect and preserve for future generations.

a our forest resources

b our fishing resources

11

The business farm

Lesson objectives

In this lesson you are going to learn about the operation of a farm as a business enterprise. On completing this lesson you should be able to:

1 Identify business farms in your village or community.

2 List the resources of a specified farm enterprise.

3 List some sources of capital for a farming enterprise.

4 State the functions of a farm manager.

5 State some ways in which farm records are helpful to a farmer.

6 Keep farm records.

7 Prepare an inventory.

8 Plan and prepare a budget for an agricultural project.

9 Assess the profitability of an agricultural project.

10 Identify market facilities in a specified locality.

11 Describe the preparation and storage of a few farm products for marketing.

In Book One we learnt that a good farmer operates the farm as a business. If you visit a farm near to your home or your school you will observe that certain resources (or inputs) are required in a business farm. The business must be well managed and there should be a ready market for the products of the farm. You will notice, too, that a successful farm brings profitable returns and provides the farmer and the employees with regular incomes.

Now try to identify a few business farms in your village or community.

The following diagram shows you the structural and operational features of a business farm. Study it carefully.

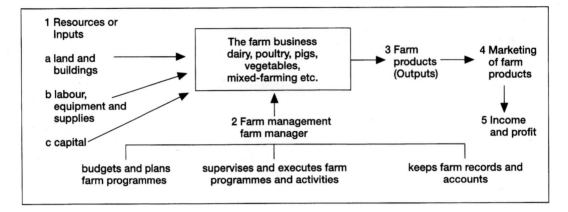

From the diagram you have just studied, you will observe that a business farm is made up of the following components.

1 Farm resources (or inputs).
2 Farm management.
3 Farm products (or outputs)
4 Marketing farm products
5 Income and profit

Resources (or inputs) of the farm

There are several types of farming and their major inputs are usually similar. However, these inputs may vary in quality and in the extent to which they are required according to the type of farm.

The photographs on this page show you a vegetable farm and a dairy farm. These farms can operate only when land, labour and capital are available.

Vegetable farm

Dairy farming

Land

1 How is land used in the two farming enterprises shown in the photographs?

2 Is the land adequate and suitable for the type of farming?

3 Is the soil fertile or is it poor?

In the farms that we are examining, you will observe the land is required for the cultivation of crops and fodder grasses, the establishment of pastures and as building sites for farmhouses. The land should be adequate and suitable and there should be good roads leading to and from the farms. Supplies of water and electricity and the location of a nearby market-place are all necessary factors in relationship to land as a farming resource.

Labour

Think about the vegetable and the dairy farms that were discussed above. Consider their labour requirements.

1 What labour operations take place on these farms?

2 Which of these operations are done

(a) **manually**, that is, by hand and with the use of simple tools and equipment and

(b) mechanically by machines?

Milking with the aid of a machine

Labour operations on a farm may be performed manually with the use of simple tools and equipment or mechanically by machines. Some operations like ploughing with a tractor or planting with a tractor-operated seeder, must be done by trained or skilled workers. However, there are many other operations which require workers with a limited amount of skill and training.

Farm workers should be healthy and energetic. They should be thoughtful, co-operative, responsible and must take a pride in their work. Good workers are always regular, punctual and gainfuly employed. Such workers should be properly remunerated for their labours and their services.

Capital

Capital is the total finance required to operate a business farm. Capital is required for fixed items such as land, buildings and machinery, and to finance the production cycle of the business from the beginning of production to the ultimate sale of the goods. The former is generally known as **fixed capital** and the latter as circulating or **working capital**.

Study the chart below. It will help you to understand this more clearly.

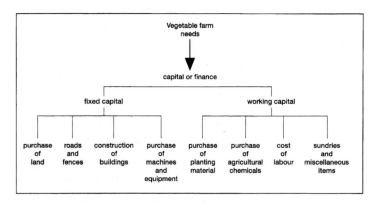

Capital needs of a vegetable farm

Sources of capital

The amount of capital required depends upon the system of farming and the intensity with which it is practised. Capital is best obtained from the savings of farm incomes. In the absence of such savings a farmer may obtain capital in the form of a loan from agricultural credit agencies such as agricultural societies, agricultural co-operatives and agricultural development banks.

Management of the Farm

If you look at a good farming enterprise, you will find that the farm resources are organised and utilised to obtain the best possible returns. The farmer or manager exercises careful control in the management of the farm during the planning, operational and financial stages. Good management ensures that all relevant records and accounts are properly kept.

Planning and budgeting

In planning the production programme, the farmer considers the available resources and decides on the items or crops to be produced, how to produce them, and how much to produce. For each programme the farmer prepares a **budget**, that is, an estimate of the expenditure envisaged and the income expected.

The table below shows you the simple budget of a farmer who intends to produce 10,000 heads of lettuce for the supermarkets. Study it carefully.

Expenditure	$	c	Income	$	c
Planting material	25	00	10 000 heads of lettuce		
Fertiliser and manures	400	00	$1.00 each	10 000	00
Pest & disease control	80	00			
Labour and transport	800	00			
Land rent	25	00			
Miscellaneous items	40	00			
Total:	1 370	00	Total:	10 000	00

You will observe that this budget indicates the items of production, the resources that are to be used and the estimated expenditure and income. A good budget often helps a farmer to secure a bank loan in order to finance future production programmes.

A farmer or manager makes several decisions in connection with the farm programmes. Labour is supervised and resources are utilised to obtain the best possible returns. Production techniques are checked that they are right.

An experienced farmer knows that many farm operations must be done at specific times and in specific ways and that the material requirements of the farm vary from project to project and from time to time. For example, a farmer will not plant lettuce seeds directly in the garden plots nor apply a fertiliser like muriate of potash to lettuce in their third week of growth.

Tell why:

1 Why should lettuce seeds *not* be planted directly in the garden plots?
2 Why is muriate of potash *not* the correct fertiliser for lettuce in its third week of growth?

Farm records and accounts

Several types of activities and transactions take place in a business enterprise. If a farmer wants to know about past farm purchases and receipts or whether the farm is making a profit, the farm **records** and accounts are consulted. These registers may vary from farm to farm. However, there are three types of records that are important on all farms.

1 The farm inventory

The farm inventory is a written record of the total assets of a farm taken at a set point in time.

Here is a inventory taken from a small broiler farm. Study it carefully.

Inventory for year ending December 31, 1994.

Item	Quantity	Unit	Estimated unit value $ c	Estimated total value $ c
Land	2.5	hectares	1 200 00	3 000 00
Farmhouse	1	each	16 000 00	16 000 00
Storehouse	1	each	4 400 00	4 400 00
Poultry houses with equipment	3	each	5 500 00	16 500 00
Lorry	1	each	25 000 00	25 000 00
Incubator	1	each	10 000 00	10 000 00
Broiler birds (8 weeks old)	3 000	each	10 80	32 400 00
Broiler birds (5 weeks old)	3 000	each	8 50	25 500 00
Broiler birds (1 week old)	3 000	each	1 80	5 400 00
Broiler starter (in stock)	100	bags	58 00	5 800 00
Broiler finisher	500	bags	56 00	28 000 00
Medication (in stock)	various	–	– –	250 00
Estimated total value:				172 250 00

This inventory gives the farmer an estimated value of the farm assets for the year ending December 31, 1994. From it, items which are present, missing or lost can be determined. It also helps the decision making on new items that should be bought for the farm.

Now try to find out how an inventory can help a farmer to determine whether or not the farm is showing growth.

2 Farm expenditure and receipts

Several types of expenditure take place on a farm during the course of its operations. Similarly, there will be many receipts from the sale of farm produce. A monthly record of farm expenditure and receipts is necessary as it assists the farmer in calculating total expenditure, total income and determining whether the farm is operating at a profit or at a loss.

Listed below is a record of the expenditure and receipts of a small pig farmer for the month of July 1994.

Expenditures and receipts for month ending July 31, 1994.

Date	Expenditure	$ c	Receipts	$ c
4.7.94	6 weaner piglets @ $80.00	480 00		
8.7.94	4 bags pig-grower ration @ 40.00	160 00		
16.7.94	4 pkt dewormer @ $8.50	34 00	2 porker pigs, total 147.5 kg live weight @ 3.00 kg	442 50
18.7.94	6 bags pig-grower @ $40.00	240 00		
24.7.94			4 porker pigs, total 290 kg live weight @3.00 kg	870 00
Total for month		914 00		1312 50

Study the farm records and find answers for the following:
1 List the items of expenditure for the month of July.
2 What is the purchasing price of a weaner piglet?
3 What is the live weight selling price of a kilo of porker pig?
4 Give the average weight of the porker pigs sold on July 24.
5 What is the difference between the total expenditure and the total receipts for the month in question?

3 Production records

Farm outputs are measured in terms of yield and quality. It is important for a farmer to keep records of the output of the various enterprises which comprise the farm.

The production records of a farm indicate to the farmer if the performance of the farm animals or the yields of the field crops are satisfactory. The farmer finds this out by making comparisons with previous farm records or with those of the neighbouring farms.

A farmer can also use the production records to decide whether to expand the existing enterprises or make changes in management practices. These records also help the farmer to determine whether to change from one enterprise to another.

Dates with Milk Production Yield (in Kilograms)									Wkly Total AM-PM	Wkly Total (kg)
Cow		1	2	3	4	5	6	7		
Mazie	AM	9.0	8.9	9.1	9.1	8.8	9.0	8.9	62.8	123.5
	PM	8.6	8.6	8.7	8.6	8.9	8.7	8.6	60.7	
Lutch-min	AM	7.1	7.1	7.0	7.2	7.2	7.3	7.1	50.0	96.3
	PM	6.6	6.7	6.6	6.5	6.7	6.5	6.7	46.3	
Bessy	AM	8.5	8.4	8.5	8.5	8.6	8.4	8.4	59.3	114.9
	PM	7.8	7.8	8.0	8.2	8.1	7.9	7.8	55.6	
Dulci	AM	8.0	8.0	8.1	8.0	7.9	8.0	8.2	56.2	108.7
	PM	7.5	7.4	7.5	7.7	7.6	7.4	7.4	52.5	
Betty	AM	6.4	6.5	6.4	6.4	6.3	6.2	6.3	44.5	87.3
	PM	6.1	6.0	6.2	6.1	6.1	6.3	6.0	42.8	
Marie	AM	9.6	9.7	9.6	9.8	9.7	9.8	9.7	67.9	130.3
	PM	8.9	8.9	9.1	9.0	9.0	8.7	8.8	62.4	

The table above shows you the milk production record of a small dairy farm for 1 week in September. Study it carefully and find out the following:

1 Which cow gave (a) the highest milk yield for the period (b) the lowest milk yield for the period?
2 Did the cows give better milk yields in the mornings or in the afternoons?
3 What was the total milk production for the period?
4 What income did the farmer make in this week if milk was sold at $1.50 per kilogram.

Products (or outputs) of the farm

Farm outputs consist of a wide range of crop and animal products. These outputs vary considerably from farm to farm, depending upon the type of farm and the yield and

fowl   goats

pigs   cattle

tomatoes   sweet-peppers

citrus   avocado-pears

the quality of farm produce. However, the ultimate aim of every farmer is to produce goods of marketable standards which take into account such factors as the production of goods and items under healthy and sanitary conditions; freedom from spoilage and physical damage and the proper **grading**, packaging and storage of goods for the markets.

Make a careful study of the table below. It tells you how a few farm products are prepared and stored for the markets.

Farm produce	Preparation and storage for the markets
1 Animal products	
Eggs	Eggs are collected daily. They are cleaned, selected and graded. They are then placed in racks and stored at a temperature of 12.8°C. They must be marketed within 7 to 8 days.
Meat	Only healthy animals are slaughtered and at the correct stage of development so as to attain the desired carcase quality. The carcase is made into market cuts and kept in cold storage.
Milk	Milk is collected from healthy animals under hygienic conditions. The milk is pasteurised, bottled and refrigerated.
2 Plant produce	
Bananas	Must be harvested at the correct stage of maturity and not bruised or damaged. They are placed in plastic bags or wrapped in straw for transport.
Tomatoes	Harvested on a dry day; place in a cupboard to ripen. When ripe, fruits are selected, graded and packed in shallow crates for the market.
Lettuce	Must be harvested in the late afternoon. Heads are washed and the old leaves are removed. They are then packed in baskets with stems upwards. The basket is kept covered with a damp muslin cloth.

Now try to find out about the preparation and storage of two other farm products for the markets.

Marketing agricultural products

Study the diagram on the next page. It will help you to understand a few simple concepts on marketing operations.

A **market** is a place where goods are bought or sold. Our farmers are the producers and the people who purchase goods from the market are the **consumers**.

In an open market, the price of goods is controlled by supply and demand, that is, the amount of goods which can be supplied by the producers and the amount of goods required by the consumer at any particular time. Now you can investigate and find out whether the market prices of cabbage will fall or rise when it is (a) in short supply and (b) plentiful (that is, in excess of market demands).

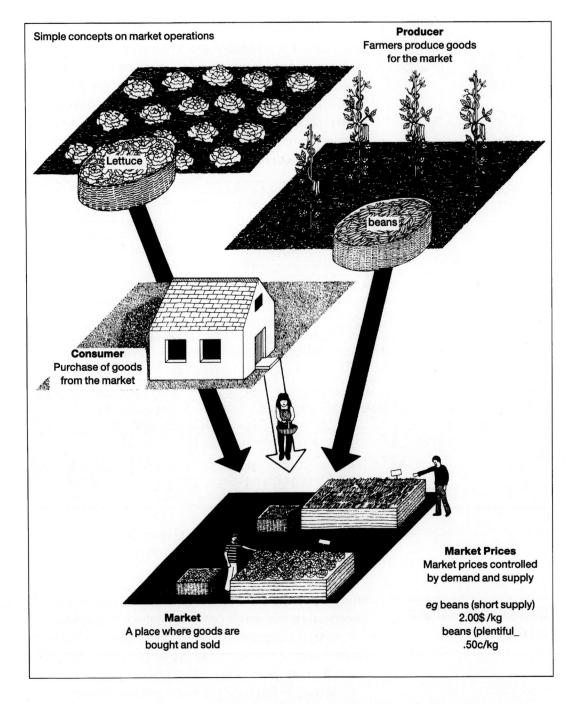

Simple concepts on market operations

Producer
Farmers produce goods
for the market

Lettuce

beans

Consumer
Purchase of goods
from the market

Market Prices
Market prices controlled
by demand and supply

eg beans (short supply)
2.00$ /kg
beans (plentiful_
.50c/kg

Market
A place where goods are
bought and sold

To maintain stable market prices, farmers must ensure that their supply of market goods is neither greater nor less than the market demands. Can you think of two reasons why the supply of cabbage could fall short or be in excess of market demands, even though the farmers may have planned their production programmes?

Marketing outlets

The marketing of farm products often begins on the farm itself. However, farmers usually market their goods on the wayside, the groceries, the district market places and at government marketing centres. Goods may also be sold to processing units and to food manufacturing agencies.

Many of our local farm products find their way into the markets of other Caribbean countries, whilst our economic crops such as coffee, cocoa, sugar-cane, bananas and citrus are sold in the foreign market.

Income and Profit on the Farm

You will remember that the income of a farm is derived from the sale of farm products. In order to obtain profits, the total income must exceed expenditure. If, however, the expenditure is greater than the income, then the farm experiences a loss. You may express this as follows:

Income less Expenditure = Profit or Loss.

For example, the expenditure on the production of a crop of lettuce is $5,500.00 and the income is $7,200.00.

$$\text{Profit or Loss} = \text{Income less Expenditure}$$
$$= 7,200.000 - 5,500.00$$
$$= \$1,700.00 \text{ (profit)}$$

Find out the profit or loss on this poultry project: The expenditure on a batch of layer birds is $8,800.00 and the income is $6,500.00.

Summary

A good farmer operates the farm as a business. The farm is managed well and the marketed products bring profitable returns. In operating a business farm, five major factors or components are taken into consideration. These are farm resources (or inputs), farm management, farm products (or outputs), marketing of farm products and the income and profits made.

Farm resources consist mainly of land, labour and capital. Land is required for crop and animal production and for the construction of farm buildings and roadways. Labour is essential for operating the farm. Capital is needed for the purchase of fixed items and for use as working capital. The amount of capital required depends upon the farming system used and the intensity of production.

In a well managed farm, the farmer or farm manager plans, budgets and executes the farm programmes. This person ensures that records are properly kept, as these help to determine whether or not the farm is operating successfully. Records are also important in planning and decision making.

The most important records on a farm are the farm inventory, the farm expenditure and receipts and the farm production records. From the farm inventory the farmer is able to determine the assets of the farm as well as the growth and developments that are taking place from time to time. The farm expenditure and receipts records help the farmer to determine if the farm is operating at a profit or a loss, whilst the production records give a measure of farm outputs in terms of yield and quality.

From a study of farm records, the farmer can make other decisions, such as changes in management practices or changes in the farming enterprise.

Farm outputs consist of a wide range of crop and animal products. These must be produced under sanitary and healthy conditions. For marketing they must be properly graded, packaged and stored.

Marketing begins on the farm itself. However, it is generally done at the groceries, the district markets, the wayside and at government marketing agencies. Goods are usually marketed in an open market system where the principle of demand and supply operates. According to the demand or supply the prices of goods may rise or fall.

Farm products are also sold to processing units, whereas economic crops are exported to foreign countries.

Remember these

Budget An estimate of the expenditure envisaged and the income expected.

Capital The total finance required to operate a business enterprise.

Consumers People who purchase goods from the market.

Fixed capital Capital required for fixed items such as land, buildings and machinery.

Grading The process of sorting out items of goods into groups of similar characteristics, e.g. size, shape, weight, colour or stage of ripening.

Inventory A written record of the total assets of an enterprise taken at a set point in time.

Manually	Done by hand with the use of simple tools.
Market	A place where goods are bought or sold.
Records	Written statements on observations, activities and transactions which take place in a business enterprise.
Working capital	Finance required for the production cycle of a business enterprise.

Practical activities

1 Visit a nearby poultry or vegetable farm and make a list of:

   a The resources or inputs of the farm and

   b The products or outputs of the farm.

2 Take an inventory of the tools and equipment used in your school vegetable garden. Use the recording sheet below:

Inventory of tools and equipment used in school vegetable garden

Name of school:

Date:

Item	Number in use on 1st day	Number at the present time	Remarks

N.B. Your teacher will give you information on 'Number in use on first day'.
Under remarks, state the condition of the tools.

State three ways in which this exercise is useful.

3 You are required to grade eggs for marketing. Do this exercise with your teacher's help. Secure the following materials and equipment: an egg grader; 2 dozen eggs; egg racks; and recording sheets. Grade the eggs and place them in the racks according to grades. Complete the records.

Date	Number of eggs graded	Grades of egg			
		small	medium	large	extra large

State the importance of this exercise to:

   a The poultry farmer and

   b The consumer.

4 Here is a project for you to undertake.

Rear 50, day-old broiler chicks at your school farm or at home. Calculate your expenditure and your income and then determine whether this project operated at a profit or at a loss. You may use the following to assist you:

Expenditure	$	c	Income (returns)	$	c
Cost of 50 day-old chicks			Sale of birds		
Total cost of feed					
Cost of medications					
Cost of labour					
Any other expenditure					
Total expenditure			**Total income**		

Calculation: Profit or Loss = Income less Expenditure

Do these test exercises

1 Select the best answer from the choices given.

a In setting up a farming business, fixed capital is required for:

A the purchase of agricultural chemicals.

B the cost of labour.

C the construction of farm buildings.

D the purchase of planting materials.

b To determine the assets of the farm, a farmer should consult the:

A farm budget

B farm inventory

C farm expenditure and receipts

D farm production records

2 What do you understand by:

a Maximum returns.

b Marketable standards.

c Economic crops.

d A skilled worker.

e Marketing outlets.

3 Differentiate between:

a Manual operations and mechanical operations.

b Fixed capital and working capital.

c Producers and consumers.

d Demand and supply.

e Expenditure and income.

4 Say how the following farm records are beneficial to a farmer:

a The farm inventory.

b Production records.

c Expenditure and income records.

5 Write a short paragraph about each of the following:

a The qualities of a good farm worker.

b The points to be borne in mind when purchasing a plot of land for vegetable cultivation.

c The duties of a farm manager.

d Price control in terms of demand and supply.

6 Make a list for each of the following:

a Sources from which farmers can obtain capital to finance their farm programmes.

b Avenues for marketing farm products.

c The resources (or inputs) of a dairy farm.

7 Say how the following farm products are prepared and stored for the market:

a eggs.

b milk.

c bananas.

d lettuce.

8 a What is a budget?

b State the factors that a farmer considers in the preparation of a budget for a production programme.

12

The role of government and other agencies in agriculture

Lesson objectives

Government and other agricultural agencies assist in the development of agriculture and agricultural education. On completing this lesson you should be able to:

1 State the role of government in the development of agriculture and agricultural education.

2 Prepare a list of non-governmental agencies that assist in agriculture and agricultural education.

3 State the functions of the Agricultural Extension Services.

4 State the objectives of each of the following:
(a) agricultural societies, (b) agricultural co-operatives and (c) agricultural development banks.

5 Explain how the 4H movement helps to make good citizens out of our boys and girls.

6 Name some agro-based industries in your country.

7 State the main aims of the United Nations organisation.

8 List the opportunities available for agricultural education in your country.

9 Identify some career opportunities in agriculture.

Agriculture is an important sector in the economy of all the Caribbean territories. The development of agriculture and agricultural education is assisted by government and by other agricultural agencies. This is done through research, **technology**, and education.

Role of government in agriculture

What role does the government play in the agriculture of your country?

The government of a country plays an important role in the development of agriculture. It formulates agricultural policies, designs agricultural programmes and enacts laws in connection with agriculture. It also grants loans and subsidies, finances research projects and assists in farm settlement schemes. Government also participates in trade agreements with other countries for the import or export of agricultural products.

Efforts are made continually to increase the number of crop and animal farms. These farms help to provide employment, to increase agricultural production and to improve the standard of living of rural people.

Now try to find out what agricultural programmes are in operation in your country in connection with any three of the following:

1 The production of vegetable crops.
2 Increasing the production of meat and milk.
3 The processing of vegetable and fruit products.
4 The production of exotic ornamental plants.
5 Soil conservation practices.
6 The development of the forest industry.
7 The production of raw materials for the animal feed industry.
8 Marketing improvements.
9 Research in crop and animal breeding.
10 The development of access roads.

Agricultural Extension Services

This picture shows you an agricultural extension officer at work. Agricultural Extension Services are sponsored by agricultural agencies such as the Ministry of Agriculture,

Advice from an Agricultural Extension Officer

commercial enterprises and private research stations. The extension department of the Ministry of Agriculture renders services to the public at large.

Agricultural Extension Services link the farming community with the research centres by means of their extension officers. These officers help farmers to solve their problems in agriculture and to assist them generally in developing their homes and their community.

Study the following diagram carefully. You will observe that extension is chiefly a process of education by which **rural communities** are developed.

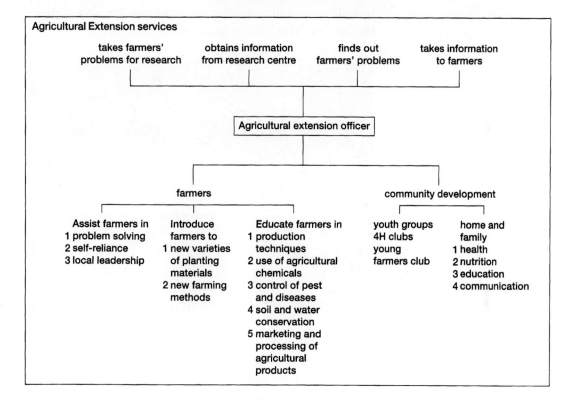

Other agricultural agencies – local and foreign

Agricultural societies and associations

Agricultural societies and associations are formed when people with common interests organise themselves and work for the benefit of their mutual agricultural interest. Agricultural societies are organised around such activities as dairy farming, bee-keeping, transport etc.

The group is well organised and operates by means of a constitution consisting of certain rules and regulations. An agricultural society keeps its members informed of recent developments in farming methods. It takes group action in planning and problem solving, and brings the views of its members to the notice of government and other agencies.

Agricultural co-operative societies

Are you a member of the junior co-operative society in your school? The junior co-operative consists of a group of pupils who work together to improve themselves financially. The members of the society subscribe money and invest it in economic projects such as the sale of exercise books, candies and soft drinks. As a result each member is entitled to an interest and a share in the surplus profits according to the amount of his/her investment.

Junior Co-operative Society

In a similar way, agicultural co-operative societies are organised by the farmers of a community. The farmers are required to invest money, to discuss, and to plan together. They save and lend money, they buy and sell agricultural items, and they share the society's work together.

Agricultural credit societies must be registered and managed according to the rules and ordinances of the co-operative sociecties of the country, but they are owned, controlled and supported by their members.

Agricultural credit or development banks

You will remember that farmers may obtain capital for agricultural development from their own savings or they may obtain loans from agricultural credit or development banks. These banks are intended to improve and increase agricultural production by granting loans and by offering technical assistance to individual farmers and to agricultural co-operative societies.

An agricultural development bank

Loans may be obtained for livestock, crops, bee-keeping, purchase of equipment and machinery, commercial fishing and for other agricultural projects of which the banks approve. Loans are usually made as short term loans, that is, for a period of 12–18 months or as medium or long term loans. Medium term loans are repaid within a period of 10 years whilst the latter may be as long as 25–30 years.

In order to obtain a loan, farmers must apply to the bank. They must give details of their agricultural programmes and the securities that they intend to offer. These are scrutinised by the bank's credit officers, and if they are satisfied, then loans are made.

4H and Young Farmers' Clubs

The 4H Club movement began in the USA and has spread to many countries of the world including the Caribbean. The aim of the 4H movement is to make good citizens out of our boys and girls. These young people are trained in the skills of good leadership and they participate in club activities which help to build their character and their self-confidence.

4H members take part in projects such as growing vegetables, rearing animals, food preparation and craft exercises. These projects provide opportunities for learning new methods in agriculture and home management.

Young farmers' clubs cater for country boys and girls between the ages of 10 and 21. The aims of these clubs are similar to those of the 4H clubs. Projects are organised to

4H club emblem

encourage members to be self-reliant, thrifty and co-operative. Members are taught improved methods of crop production and livestock management and the economic values of such practices.

Young farmers

Agro-industrial interests

You will observe that agriculture is the hub around which other industries revolve. Some of these industries support agriculture, while others depend upon agriculture.

Agro-based industries promote agriculture in several ways. They grant financial aid and offer technical assistance to agricultural projects. They conduct agricultural research and training programmes and provide employment opportunities for many people.

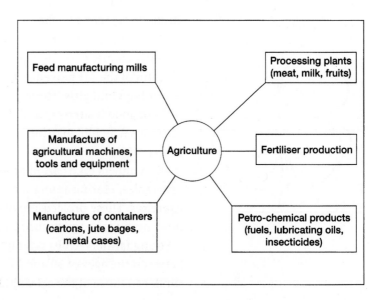

Agro-based industries

Caribbean Agricultural Research and Development Institute (CARDI)

CARDI has its headquarters at the University of the West Indies, St Augustine, Trinidad. This institute serves 12 member countries of the Caribbean and its aim is to contribute to agricultural development through the generation and dissemination of appropriate technology that benefits the Caribbean people.

The institute is actively engaged in research and development work on crop production and livestock management programmes. It is also involved in non-traditional crops including ornamentals, fruits and *Aloe vera*.

Improved meat production – Blackbelly sheep

The information obtained from research along with the development of new technologies are passed on to the national Extension Service of the member territories for implementation.

Caribbean Industrial Research Institute (CARIRI)

CARIRI is also located at the University of the West Indies campus, St Augustine. The aim of this institute is 'to advance the economic and social development of Trinidad and Tobago and other countries in the Caribbean region by providing technical and technological support and creating and transferring technology to the producers of goods and services'.

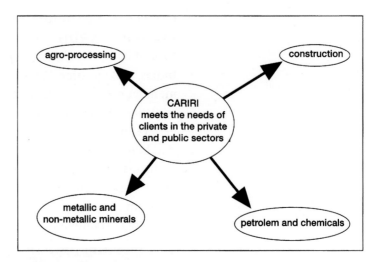

Technical information
branches of CARIRI

In the field of agro-processing, extensive work is conducted in product and process development and in contract processing. In addition, the institute offers services in consultancy, testing and training.

You should now be able to identify some agro-industries in your country.

United Nations organisations

The United Nations (UN) is an international organisation which was founded in 1945 and now consists of over 90 sovereign nations. The main aims of the UN are to maintain international peace and security; to observe the principles of respect and equal rights for all humanity; and to promote social progress and better standards of life for all people.

Within the UN, there are smaller councils or agencies, whose functions are to promote agriculture, health and education. They make funds available and provide technical aid to educational and agricultural projects.

United Nations Educational, Scientific and Cultural Organisation (UNESCO)

UNESCO seeks to promote collaboration among the nations through education, science and culture.

UNESCO is concerned with such agricultural problems as pollution of the sea; water supply and irrigation schemes; agricultural education in schools and for the farming community; supplies of agricultural materials, tools and equipment and the training of teachers.

UNESCO headquarters

Food and Agricultural Organisation (FAO)

FAO was established in 1946. It seeks to improve the living standards and raise the nutritional levels of people throughout the world. It offers technical assistance by sending experts to developing countries to advise them on how to grow more food and crops; how to control pests and diseases in plants and animals, how to protect food in storage and how to increase yields of farms, fisheries and forests.

Now try and find out if UNESCO and/or FAO operate in your island or country; and how these agencies assist in educational and agricultural programmes.

Organisation of American States (OAS)

The OAS was formally established in 1948 at Bogata in Columbia. Its prime objectives are to offer technical services to members in economic, legal and cultural fields.

There is close co-operation with the OAS and corresponding UN agencies. The OAS is also affiliated to the Inter-American Development Bank founded in 1959 to provide capital for private and public projects in the American Republics including the Caribbean.

Education and career opportunities in agriculture

Agricultural science is taught in many primary and secondary schools of the Caribbean. It is also offered as an elective subject at the CXC 'O' Level examination. Beyond this, students may pursue agriculture at technical institutes or at universities.

Students with a primary school leaving certificate, as well as students from the junior and senior secondary school system find their way into youth camps, farm schools and agriculture **apprenticeship schemes** to be trained as agricultural craftsmen. They are able to take care of their own private farms or to obtain employment as agricultural workers and junior supervisors on other farms.

Students entering agricultural institutes and colleges must possess five 'O' Level passes with grades I or II in mathematics, English and a science subject. These students graduate as agricultural technicians and are trained to fill the positions of agricultural assistants and foresters in government service. They also serve as managers in commercial agricultural firms and as agricultural science teachers in schools and colleges.

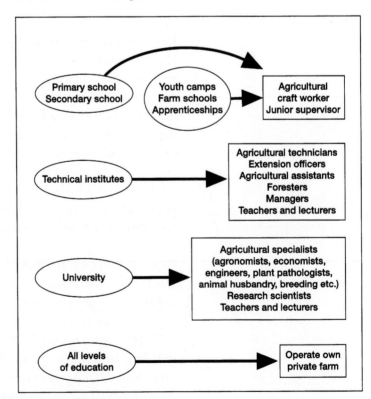

Education and career in opportunities

Students who wish to pursue agriculture at the universities must have 'A' level passes in at least 2 or 3 subjects along with 'O' level passes as entry requirement. At the universities, agricultural studies are pursued at graduate and post-graduate level. Such graduates are employed as agronomists, animal specialists, agricultural economists, agricultural engineers, plant pathologists, plant and animal breeders, teachers, lecturers and research scientists in various fields of agriculture.

You too, have opportunities for an education and career in agriculture. Are you preparing yourself for these opportunities and for one of these careers in agriculture?

Summary

Agriculture and agricultural education are developed and assisted by government and by other agricultural agencies. Government formulates agricultural policies, design agricultural programmes and enacts laws in connection with agriculture. Government also grants loans and subsidies, finances research projects, assists in farm settlement schemes and participates in trade agreements with other countries.

Government policies are carried out by the Ministry of Agriculture through planned programmes and activities conducted mainly by the extension services. Personnel from the extension department help farmers to solve their problems in agriculture and assist them generally in developing their homes and their communities.

Some other agencies involved in the development of agriculture are agricultural societies, agricultural co-operatives and agricultural credit banks. An agricultural society is organised by farmers with mutual agricultural interests. The society takes group action in helping farmers with planning and problem solving. It also provides its members with activities and opportunities for social and community development.

Agricultural co-operatives help farmers to improve themselves financially by encouraging them to invest and participate in economic projects. The surplus or profits from such projects make finance available to the members of the co-operative.

Agricultural credit banks assist farmers with loans and technical assistance for approved agricultural projects.

Loans are usually made as short term, medium term or long term loans depending on the nature of the project for which the loan is granted.

Useful work is also done for the young people of rural communities. They are encouraged to participate in 4H clubs and young farmers organisations. These organisations help to train young boys and girls in the skills of good agricultural practices and leadership by involving them in activities.

Agriculture is the hub of several agro-based industries. These industries support agriculture or depend upon agriculture for their support. Agro-based industries promote agriculture by granting financial aid and by offering technical assistance. They also conduct research and training programmes and provide employment opportunities for people. In the Caribbean, extensive work is done by CARDI and CARIRI in the field of agricultural research and agro-based industries.

One of the aims of the UN is to promote agriculture, health and education. This is done through funding and technical assistance by the UN agencies of UNESCO and FAO. The OAS also supports agriculture in the Caribbean and works in close co-operation with the UN.

There are several educational and career opportunities in agriculture. Students graduating from youth camps and farm schools are generally employed as craftsman whilst those graduating from agricultural institutes and colleges find career opportunities as technicians, teachers and managers. University graduates are qualified for career activities ranging from specialists in the areas of crop and animal husbandry to research scientists in various aspects of agricultural production.

Remember these

Agro-based industries	Industries which support agriculture or which depend upon agriculture for support.
Agricultural co-operative society	A group of people who organise themselves and work together to improve themselves financially by subscribing money and investing in agricultural projects of economic value.
Agricultural development bank	Banks intended to improve and increase agricultural production by granting loans and by offering technical

assistance to individual farmers and to agricultural co-operative societies.

Agricultural extension service
An arm of the Ministry of Agriculture involved in a process of education by which rural communities are developed.

Agricultural policy
Course of action adopted by government in connection with agriculture and agricultural development.

Agricultural society
A group of people who organise themselves and work for the benefit of their mutual agricultural interest.

Apprenticeship scheme
A scheme in which the learner of a craft is bound to the employer for a specific term designed especially for training.

Rural communities
Countryside communities that are closely linked with agriculture for their support and development.

Technology
The application of science for practical value in industrial and agricultural uses.

United Nations
An international organisation consisting of over 90 sovereign nations. The main objective of this organisation is to maintain international peace and to promote social progress and better standards of life for all people.

Practical activities

1 Visit the agricultural extension office in your district and have a discussion with the agricultural extension officer about his duties.

2 Ask your teacher to invite an officer of the agricultural credit bank to one of your class sessions and investigate the following:

   a The objectives of the agricultural credit bank.

   b The purposes for which loans are granted.

   c The types of loan granted by the bank.

   d The conditions under which loans are granted.

   e The monitoring of loans to ensure that they are utilised correctly.

3 Collect the programme of activities pursued by the members of a 4H club.

   a State the skills that will be learnt by the members of the club.

   b Explain how these skills could make good citizens out of our boys and girls.

4 Visit a few nearby agro-based industries.

   a Which of these industries support agriculture?

   b Name the industries that depend upon agriculture for support.

Do these test exercises

1 **Select the best answer from the choices given.**

a Which of these is NOT a function of government?

  A formulating agricultural policies.

  B designing agricultural programmes.

  C providing labour for farmers.

  D finance research projects.

b A farmer requiring information on agro-processing should consult:

  A CARIRI

  B CARDI

  C UNESCO

  D FAO

c An agricultural development bank loan is considered medium term if it is taken for a period of:

  A 1 to 1 1/2 years

  B 3 to 5 years

  C 8 to 10 years

  D 25 to 30 years

d A crop showed poor growth and development; to solve this problem the farmer is best advised to consult:

  A The Food and Agricultural Organisation

  B The Organisation of American States

  C The agricultural co-operative society

  D The Agricultural Extension Services

2 **State the role that the government of a country plays in the development of agriculture.**

3 **State some ways in which the Agricultural Extension Services help in community development.**

4 **List some ways in which an agricultural society is beneficial to farmers.**

5 **Explain to a farmer the benefits that are gained by becoming a member of an agricultural co-operative society.**

6 **State the aims of:**

a The Caribbean Agricultural Research and Development Institute (CARDI).

b The Caribbean Industrial Research Institute (CARIRI).

c The Food and Agricultural Organisation (FAO).

7 **Identify 12 career opportunities that are available in agriculture.**

13

Some new technologies and developments in agriculture

Lesson objectives

On completing this lesson you should be able to:

1 Identify a few new technologies and developments in agriculture.

2 Explain the principle on which a hydroponic system operates.

3 Explain the concept of plant reproduction by means of tissue culture.

4 State the advantages and disadvantages of plant reproduction by tissue culture.

5 Prepare a list of ornamental plants and flowers grown for the local industry and for export.

6 Describe the establishment and management practices of any two of the ornamental plants and flowers listed in objective (5) above.

7 List the functions of a computer as a management tool in a farming enterprise.

Research and experimental work in agriculture have given rise to new technologies and developments in agricultural production.

These new technologies and developments are passed on to the farming community through various agricultural organisations but more so by the Agricultural Extension Services.

Let us consider some agricultural trends and practices now carried out in a few of our Caribbean territories.

Hydroponic food production

Hydroponics is the science of growing plants in a soilless medium.

Tomato production by hydroponics

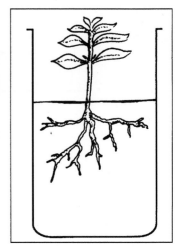

Basil plant growing in nutrient solution

The picture at the right shows a basil plant growing in a nutrient solution. This is a simple method but demonstrates the principle of hydroponic plant production. You will observe that the roots are submerged in a solution from which they absorb nutrient supplies for the plant.

The picture below shows you how lettuce can be grown in a nutrient solution. Study it carefully.

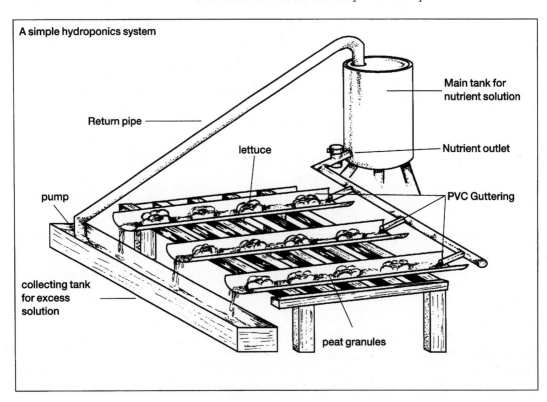

A simple hydroponics system

Lettuce seedlings are sown in peat pellets and placed into the PVC guttering. Nutrient solution in controlled amounts is allowed to flow through the guttering from which the lettuce obtains its nutrient requirements. The excess solution is directed into a collecting tank and then pumped into the main tank with the new nutrient solution for recycling.

Under commercial greenhouse production the plants are generally grown in an inert medium such as sand, gravel, peat or vermiculite to which is added a nutrient solution containing all the essential elements needed by plants for normal growth and development. Under this system a wide variety of vegetable crops, such as tomato, lettuce, patchoi, cabbage, celery, beans and cucumbers, are produced.

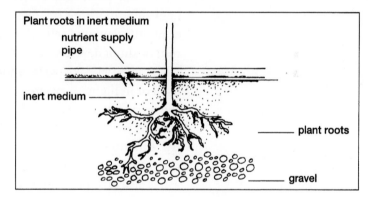

Crops grown in greenhouses need special care and attention. The farmer must ensure that light and temperature conditions are adequate and the nutrient supply must contain all the essential elements for the particular crop that is grown. A high level of sanitation and crop protection must be maintained.

If you look around, you will notice that not many farmers enter into greenhouse crop production. Do you know why? It is because greenhouses are very costly to establish and agricultural chemicals are very expensive. The farmer also has to be a very skilled person to produce crops in a greenhouse.

Plant tissue culture

Plant tissue culture is the technique of reproducing plants from small portions of plant tissues grown on an artificial medium. The process is carried out under sterile conditions and in a controlled environment. The artificial medium is either a liquid or a gel. The medium contains all the mineral elements and vitamins necessary for plant growth along with an energy source such as carbohydrate and the plant growth regulators auxins and cytokinins.

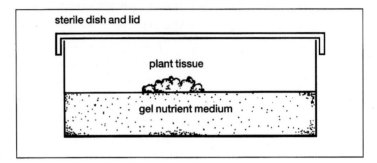

sterile dish and lid

plant tissue

gel nutrient medium

Plant tissue culture

For some plants and where the two growth regulators are in even proportions cell division takes place to form a mass of undifferentiated cells, that is, cells which do not show root or shoot development. These cells are called callus.

Changes will take place in the plant tissue if auxin is by itself or in higher concentration than cytokinin to induce the formation of roots whilst cytokinin by itself or in higher concentration than auxin will induce shoot formation. By regulating the composition of the medium, a new plant can be developed from callus to plantlet.

It is also possible, with some plants, to develop embryo-like structures, that is, structures that give rise to roots and shoots .

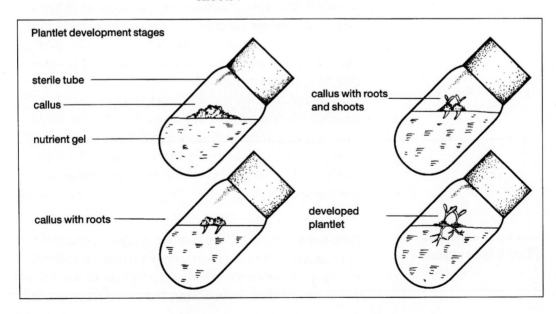

Plantlet development stages

sterile tube

callus

nutrient gel

callus with roots

callus with roots and shoots

developed plantlet

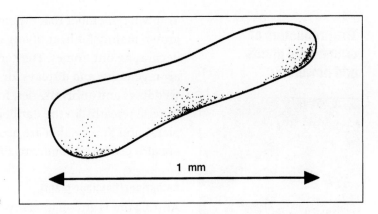

Embryo–like structure

When embryo-like structures are used, the entire plant is produced in a single step.

Many commercial laboratories now produce plants solely by tissue culture. Some species, such as orchids and Anthuriums, are now produced principally by tissue culture techniques.

Advantages and disadvantages of tissue culture

Advantages

1 Many plants can be produced from a small portion of plant tissue in very small space. This makes tissue culture economical as far as space is concerned.
2 Depending on the technique used the plant can be true to type, that is, identical to the parent plant.
3 Tissue culture can allow for the elimination of disease including disease caused by viruses.
4 Tissue culture does not depend on weather conditions since it is all carried out in the laboratory.

Disadvantages.

1 The techniques involved in tissue culture require skilled labour. There are not many people with such skills.
2 The equipment used is very expensive. Many people cannot afford to purchase them.
3 The plants are initially very small and since they are produced in a controlled environment, they require a long period of hardening before they could be put under normal field conditions.
4 Since many plants are produced from a single piece of tissue, it is possible to get off-type plants, that is, plants that are a little different from the parent plant.

The production of ornamental plants and flowers.

Floral arrangement

Anthurium (Flamingo plant)

Anthurium potted in a coconut husk

You will remember that ornamental plants and flowers are grown mainly for beautifying our surroundings and decorating our homes. They are also required for making arrangements and displays for such occasions as birthdays, weddings and anniversaries, for corsages or for making funeral wreaths. In the Caribbean, there are many exotic plants and flowers that are used for these purposes. They are also produced commercially for export.

Anthurium (flamingo plant)

Anthurium is grown in many home ornamental plots as well as in large plantations by a few farmers. There are several varieties of Anthurium but the most popular colours are the flamingo red, the pink and the white. There are also a number of hybrid types with very large flowers and colours of different shades.

The plant could be grown from seeds, but it is generally propagated by division, that is, taking a cluster of plants and dividing it into single plants for planting.

Anthurium thrives well in the tropics. It requires semi-shaded conditions with high levels of moisture around its roots. To maintain this moisture supply, the remains of coconut husk and rotted wood are usually placed around the roots and watered regularly. The plant is kept free from weeds, dried leaves are removed and artificial fertiliser applications are made periodically. In a cluster, only two or three plants are allowed to develop. As a result, reasonably large flowers are produced. Blooms are collected throughout the year, but they are most abundant soon after the rainy season begins.

Orchids

A wide range of tropical orchids are found in the Caribbean. They produce spikes with blooms of high value. The flowers are widely used in the preparation of corsages, arrangements and wreaths. They also fetch a high price in the export market. Among the many orchids in cultivation, the most popular are Cattleya, Dendrobium and Vanda. There are also many hybrid types in cultivation.

Orchids are generally propagated by vegetative means. For example, Cattleyas are propagated by division, Dendrobiums from buds or plantlets produced on the flower stem and Vandas from stem cuttings in which aerial

Cattelya orchid

Dendrobium orchid

Vanda orchid

roots are present. Orchids could also be propagated from seeds, but this has to be done in a special medium. The process is very slow and requires the services of a skilled person.

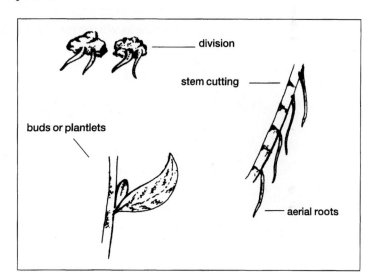

Orchid propagation

Orchids are usually grown in perforated clay pots, wooden baskets and on portions of tree stems. Orchids grown in pots or wooden baskets require a potting medium consisting of a specially prepared compost or peat moss. Gravel, larva rocks, charcoal and wood chips are also included in the pots and baskets.

Some orchids, like Cattleyas and Vandas, are light loving and they do well in the open. Dendrobiums need semi-shaded conditions and are usually grown in orchid houses covered with sarran netting. Other management practices include watering under dry conditions, control of pests and

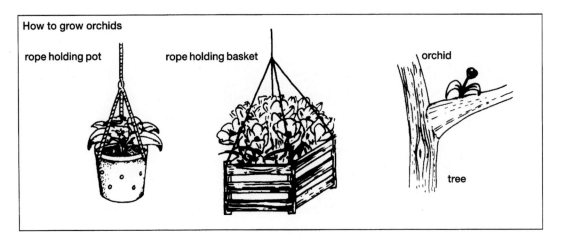

How to grow orchids

rope holding pot   rope holding basket   orchid

tree

diseases and the periodic application of a foliar spray which is made up of a weak solution of a well balanced fertiliser such as 20.20.20.

Blooms are generally collected when most of the flower buds on a spike are open. They are secured in plastic sheets for sale locally or for export. Their shelf life varies according to the species and the method of storage employed.

Ginger Lily

The chief varieties of Ginger Lily grown are the red and the pink. The plant is usually propagated from suckers or from plantlets, that is, little plants which develop from small buds on the old blooms.

Land preparation involves ploughing, incorporation of organic manure and proper drainage. It must be remembered that Ginger Lily needs a lot of water but cannot withstand waterlogging. Plants are usually placed in rows 3–3.5 m apart and 2.5–3 m within the rows. Aftercare practices include irrigation during the dry season, weed control, the removal of unwanted shoots, control of cluster size and the monthly application of a fertiliser such as 12.12.17.2.

Blooms are harvested as they are required. The stalks are generally cut close to the ground, which promotes the quick production of new shoots. The flowers are then cleaned, graded and packaged for the local market or for export.

Ginger Lily

Heliconia

There are several varieties of Heliconia in cultivation. However, the most popular ones are Golden Torch, Sexy

Heliconia

Pink and the Bahai types. Heliconia belongs to the banana family of plants. It is propagated by suckers.

Land preparation involves ploughing, incorporation of organic manures and good drainage. Spacings is dependent on the variety: 3–3.5 m between rows and 2–2.5 metres within the rows. General care and management is similar to that of Ginger Lily. To obtain good quality blooms, it is essential to control the size of the clusters by pruning all unwanted shoots. There should be optimum sunlight and adequate supplies of water.

Like Ginger Lily, blooms are harvested when required. The stem is cut near to the soil and the flowers are cleaned, graded and packaged for the market. It must be noted that the blooms of some species of Heliconia deteriorate rapidly and delays after harvesting could be detrimental to the flowers.

Computers in agriculture

Many of our farming and marketing enterprises use computers in their operations. A computer is a machine that is capable of accepting data and instructions. It performs some operations on the data and makes the results available to use in the management of the enterprise. A computer can be set up as a single unit at a station or it may be linked through a server system, that is a connecting system, to other stations.

A computer station

Computers are designed to perform several functions. They do this with great speed and accuracy. On a farm, computers are used for storing farm records and information. They make computations, analyse data and assist in solving problems. By means of the computer, a farmer quickly determines whether the farm is operating successfully or not. The farmer is also able to make decisions in connection with the development and future operations of the farm.

Summary

New technologies and developments in agriculture are passed on to the farming community mainly through the Agricultural Extension Services of a country. In this chapter we looked at five new practices in the Caribbean.

Hydroponics is the science of growing plants in a soilless medium and providing a nutrient solution containing all the essential elements. Under this system, a wide range of vegetable crops can be grown. In commercial greenhouse production, the crops are generally grown on an inert medium to which is added the nutrient solution. Few farmers carry out greenhouse crop production, because greenhouses are costly to establish, agricultural chemicals are expensive, and the farmer also has to be a skilled person to produce crops in a greenhouse.

Plant tissue culture is the technique of reproducing plants from small portions of plant tissue on an artificial medium. The medium contains essential mineral elements and the growth regulators auxins and cytokinins. These growth regulators are responsible for cell division, and the development of roots and shoots to ultimately form a small plant.

The major advantages of tissue culture propagation are the production of many plants from a small portion of tissue, eliminating virus diseases and reproducing plants true to type. Among the disadvantages, the major ones are the high cost of equipment needed for this technique and the length of time required to produce a plant.

Ornamental plants and flowers are used for decorations and for making corsages, floral arrangements and wreaths. They are grown for local use as well as for export. Among the wide range of exotic plants grown for ornamental purposes, the most popular are Anthurium, Orchids,

Ginger Lily, Heliconia and foliage plants, such as Croton and Dracaena. These plants need proper care and management including such cultivation practices as the correct propagation technique, land preparation, irrigation, pest and disease control and fertiliser application. It must be noted that the blooms of many ornamental plants are delicate: they must be harvested, graded and packaged with great care.

Computers are used in many agricultural enterprises. These machines perform operations with great speed and accuracy. They store farm records and information, make computations, analyse data and assist a farmer in solving problems and making decisions. The computer also helps a farmer to determine if the farm is operating successfully or not.

Remember these

Callus	Mass of undifferentiated plant cells formed in tissue culture.
Corsage	A flower or flowers worn on bodice or shoulder.
Foliage plants	Plants grown especially for their leaves.
Hydroponics	The science of growing plants in a soilless medium.
Inert	Free from chemicals.
Spike	A number of flowers on a long common axis.
Tissue culture	The technique of reproducing plants from small portions of plant tissue.
True to type	Identical to the parent plant.

Practical activities.

1 Fill two clay pots, labelled A and B, with coarse river sand. Plant lettuce seedlings in pots A and B and water regularly. Apply a nitrogenous fertiliser to pot A once per week.

Observe the plant growth at the end of three weeks. Comment on the plant growth in pots A and B. State reasons for differences you may have observed.

2 Visit a nearby flower shop.
   a Prepare a list of local flowers used in the flower shop.
   b State the ways in which the flowers are used.

3 Collect blooms of orchids, Anthurium, Ginger Lily and Heliconia. Place them in vases with water. Remember to top up or change the water every day.

Complete the table below:

Ornamental plant	Length of time bloom can last in a vase
Orchid	
Anthurium	
Ginger Lily	
Heliconia	

How is this information useful to a farmer?

4 Use the guide lines given in this lesson and establish a small cluster of one of the following in your school ornamental plot: Ginger lily; Anthurium; Heliconia.

Do these test exercises

1 Select the best answer from the choices given.

a Heliconias are propagated by

A divisions

B suckers

C plantlets

D stem cuttings

b Vanda is a variety of

A Heliconia

B Ginger Lily

C Anthurium

D Orchid

c In tissue culture root development is induced by

A cytokinins

B auxins

C equal concentrations of cytokinins and auxins

D higher concentrations of cytokinins than auxins

d Which statements are correct about greenhouse crop production?

(i) It is very costly to establish greenhouses.

(ii) Agricultural chemicals for use in greenhouses are expensive.

(iii) Skilled persons are needed for greenhouse crop production.

A (i) and (ii) only

B (i) and (iii) only

C (ii) and (iii) only

D (i), (ii) and (iii) are all correct.

2 List six vegetable crops that can be produced in a greenhouse.

3 State the advantages and disadvantages or propagating plants by tissue culture.

4 Describe how you will establish and take care of a plot of Ginger Lily.

5 Explain how a computer is useful to a farmer in the operation of his farm.

Appendix 1:   Safe use of agricultural chemicals

Here are some points to remember in the safe use of agricultural chemicals.

1. Select and use the correct chemical for the desired purpose. The manufacturer's instructions must be followed.
2. When more than one chemical is used in preparing a mixture ensure that the chemicals are compatible, that is, the chemicals would not affect each other in the mixture.
3. Use proper clothing and safety equipment such as a respirator, gloves, goggles, tall boots and head cover for spraying.
4. Ensure that spraying equipment is free from leaks and is working satisfactorily.
5. Spraying is best done in the early morning hours or late evenings when it is not very windy. During the spraying process, the operator's back should be against the wind.
6. Eating, drinking or smoking must be avoided during spraying.
7. All unused mixtures must be properly disposed of in a pit where it can cause no harm or pollution to the environment.
8. After spraying the operator should wash with soap and water and possibly take a bath before attempting to eat or drink.
9. Empty containers which had chemicals must not be put into other use. They should be buried or burnt.
10. All agricultural chemicals should be properly stored in a locked cupboard.
11. There must be an adequate time lapse between the last spraying and harvesting of crop.
12. If chemical poisoning is suspected, the person affected should be rushed to a doctor or hospital immediately. Evidence of the chemical used should also be taken along, e.g. the empty container.

Appendix 2:

Safety practices in the forestry industries

Here are some safety practices that should be observed by people engaged in the forestry industries.

Safety for people in forestry

1 Provide yourself with a map or a diagram which shows the location of the forest and other associated features such as roadways, tracks and rivers.

2 Timber and lumber workers must be careful when carrying and using their tools and equipment.

3 Be conscious of the presence of wild animals, snakes and vermins. These may be dangerous.

4 When making a forest tour, it is advisable to travel in organised groups with a guide to direct and assist.

5 Holiday makers or hikers in the forest should equip themselves with a compass, a portable radio, a flash light and possibly a telecommunication system.

6 Be on the alert for hunters or for illegally set trap-guns during the open season.

7 Avoid hunting or other sporting activities during the closed season. If caught you will be prosecuted.

8 Abide by the rules which govern and operate the forest industry.

Index